The emergence of the Music Critic in late 18th century London: Composers, Performers, Reporters

by Sarah J. Wynn

LANGFORD & ASSOCIATES
MEMPHIS

The emergence of the Music Critic in late 18th century London: Composers, Performers, Reporters.

by Sarah J. Wynn

Thank you:
        Dr. Elmo Howell
        Dr. Carol Fruchtman
        Dr. Efrim Fruchtman
        Mrs. Ethel T. Maxwell
        Dr. Binford Peeples

In Memoriam
to
Larry

PUBLICATIONS

Sarah Wynn, "Karl Friedrich Abel---Some Contemporary Impressions," Journal of the Viola da Gamba Society of America, no. 10 (1973): 5-10

Sarah Wynn, "The London Music Scene, 1785-1789, as reflected in *The Times,*" American Music Teacher 33, no. 4 (February-March, 1984): 36-41

Sarah Wynn, "The London Music Scene, 1785-1789: The Critic and Stage Music," American Music Teacher 37, no. 2 (November-December, 1986): 36-38

Sarah Wynn, "The London Music Scene, Italian Opera and the Critic, 1785-1789," The Music Review 53, no. 2 (May, 1992): 75-82

CONTENTS

Italian Opera and the Critic
1785-1789

John Walter, in the 1780's, suffered serious business misfortunes in the coal market and other ventures but, undaunted, he turned his energies and his professional interest in book-printing and publishing to a new venture, the daily newspaper — itself a relative newcomer to English journalism. On January 1, 1785, the first issue of Walter's four-page paper appeared on the streets and in the coffee-houses of London under the name *The Daily Universal Register*. Its very first columns vividly reflect the activities of this busy, thriving metropolis and its energetic music scene. This study — this sampling from the years 1785-1789 — of the newly established paper, later to be called *The Times* (March 17, 1788), indicates, from its beginning, the enthusiasm for music and the abundance and variety of music activities in the city and its environs. Indeed, in the early days of his paper, (January 2, 1786 p.2) John Walter announced that "the Italian Opera, Oratorio, every concert and other Musical Meeting of reputation shall be attended to," and he promised that "every source shall be explored for intelligence, entertainment and information of every species."[1]

Many kinds of musical activities were going on in London and elsewhere during the period 1785-1789. For example, reflect-

1

ing the great choral tradition were the frequent oratorio concerts and performances and festivals in the city and in the provinces. There were countless orchestral performances. Haydn in his two lengthy visits to London in the early 1790's (June, 1791 and August, 1795) was so smitten by the excellence of the impressive Hanover Square Concerts (as the Londoners were by him) that he was inspired to write his twelve great London symphonies. Rounding out the music scene were innumerable other instrumental activities brought into focus by the various subscription series, by countless "benefits" and by concerts in the private halls of the nobility and the wealthy. Small organizations, the music "clubs," the Anacreontic Society, the Pantheon Concerts, and the Freemason Concerts vied for the attention of music audiences. All were reported in *The Times* with regularity.

One of the most engaging and most colourful aspects of the scene was, of course, the Italian Opera at the King's Theatre, where operas were regularly performed. London's interest in and access to Italian opera were traditional, dating from mid-seventeenth century. Accounts of the early importations of music and performers are many, and the diverse reactions to the successes and failures in production and in performance are found in histories, essays and memoirs of contemporary figures such as music historian Dr. Charles Burney and such literary figures as John Evelyn, Samuel Pepys and Joseph Addison, whose incisive wit and satirical comments on Italian opera are classic.

Similarly, responses to Italian opera at the end of the eighteenth century were marked with friendliness and great admiration as well as "habit-of-mind," and also, of course, with some animosity and scorn. Indeed, Italian singers were a frequent subject for essays, letters and green-room gossip in the columns of *The Daily Universal Register*. Evidence indicates that the English still welcomed these artists to their stage and that the English enthusiasm for their art encouraged them to visit, to give concerts, to teach and to remain in residence for long periods of time. The young *London Times* repeatedly brought to its readers news of such composers as Cherubini, Cimarosa, Piccini, Jomelli, Paisiello, Anfossi, Tarchi, Sarti, Salieri, Traetta and Rauzzini.

Among dozens of singers of Italian opera who found great favor with London audiences at this time were Signoras Sestini, Todi, Schinotti, Georgi, Ferraresi, Banti, and Madame Mara, who won high acclaim in Germany and France and was enormously admired in England for her virtuosity and great personal charm. Male singers frequently mentioned in the new London paper were Crescentini, Rubinelli, Marchesi, Bartolini, Cremonini and Pacchierotti. The names of these and many other virtuosi are found in the news day after day, and the enthusiastic accounts of their performances in opera, oratorio and concert attest to the sophisticated interest of and continuing support by Londoners in the latter part of the eighteenth century.

On Saturday, January 15, 1785, the two-week-old *Daily Universal Register* carried its first announcement for the King's Theatre opera, *Demetrio*. It was advertised as "a serious opera in two acts, the music selected from the most eminent composers by and under the direction of Signor Cherubini." Surprisingly, however, while all other musical activities were amply covered by the paper, there is no further reference to this opera and, furthermore, there is neither announcement nor mention in the *D.U.R.* of any other Italian opera during the entire year. This Winter-Spring season did not seem to be a good one for aspiring opera enthusiasts and preceded a summer when, according to Burney, "the whole opera machine came to pieces, and all its springs, disordered by law suits, warfare, and factions (problems which seem to have plagued its history from early in the century) were not collected and regulated till the next year."[2]

A new era for Italian opera in London did indeed begin auspiciously that next year according to the *D.U.R.'s* account, with the production of a Paisiello comic opera, *Il Marchesi Tulipano*, on January 24, 1786. The fortunate turn of events seems to have been due to two organizational changes: Wilhelm Cramer became the permanent director of the band (*i.e.* the orchestra), and one

Giovanni Andrea Battista Gallini, later knighted and called Sir John Gallini, became manager of the King's Theatre.

Much of the record of the opera from 1785 to 1789 revolves about the activities of this *entrepreneur extraordinaire*. Biographical details indicate that, born in Florence in 1728, he emigrated to England in his youth. Almost destitute, he made his *debut* at the opera house as a ballet dancer, began to acquire some reputation as a dancing master and became a principal dancer before becoming the manager of the King's Theatre. Burney thought ill of this man, referring to him as "Mr. Gallini invested with the power of ruining himself and others."[2] Allusions by others hint of similar reactions. *The Daily Universal Register* reflects much of the controversy that swirled about Gallini, even while he was giving new direction to serious opera. The paper repeatedly reports the feuds in which he engaged with the actors, singers and dancers, with other managers and with governing bodies, and, particularly, with the Lord Chamberlain, whose power it was to grant theatre licenses. Neverthless, it seems from the accounts in *The Times* that he was a hard, practical business man, energetic and resourceful. With or without scruples, constantly in contact with activities on the Continent, he was able to bring to London the best talent from Italy and to offer the London audience singers of the first rank and dancers from the most prestigious ballets in France. The *D. U. R.* (May 2, 1785, p.2) announced that "Mr. Gallini has made several capitol engagements, in the singing and dancing lines, and certainly intends to bring forward an Italian opera next winter." Gallini wasted no time. Gambling on success, he apparently went into the winter season on a "no cure, no pay" basis (September 23, 1785 p.2). He did not fail, of course. The Court of Chancery approved and confirmed the agreement, and the Lord Chamberlain finally granted his license. Closing the year on an optimistic note for good things to come, the paper on December 31, (p.3) was sure that, "under the auspices of Gallini, we may expect the opera to flourish."

And so with the production of Paisiello's comic opera *Il Marchesi Tulipano* on January 24, 1786, under the direction of Cherubini and with Wilhelm Cramer as director of the band, the new era did begin with great promise. Anfossi was well represented this year (1786) by the presentation of his *Didone Abbandonata* and his *L'Inglese in Italia*, which were mildly received. His *I Viaggiatori Felici*, however, prompted a green-room reporter's attack — not distinguished for its subtlety: "with scarcely any *per contra* by way of litigation, a viler opera, we never heard" (May 30, 1786, p. 2). Other composers represented in the same year were Salieri, Mortellari and Tarchi, whose *Virginia* was responsible for Rubinelli's first appearance in England. Rubinelli's immediate popularity probably accounted for the long run of this opera for ten performances in 1786 and for its revival in 1787 for

6

six performances.

The 1786-1787 winter season opened with Gresnich's *Alceste*, which was composed for Madame Mara. Produced on December 23rd and again on December 30th, it ran for nine performances until March 8th. It was apparently a dull opera, however, and only because of the "wonderful powers of Mara and Rubinelli" did it continue, *The Times* (February 8, 1787, p.3) said, "to drag out its miserable existence." In January, Cimarosa's comic opera *Giannina e Bernardone* and Rauzzini's serious opera *La Vestale* appeared. A major attraction in the spring was the presentation of Handel's *Giulio Cesare in Egitto* "entirely under the direction of Dr. Arnold." It was staged first as a benefit on March 1, 1787 and again on March 3rd as a regular performance. The public enjoyed eleven presentations, but only one, the first, was reviewed. As always *The Times* response (March 5, 1787, p.2), to the magic name of Handel was eulogistic: "The triumph of Caesar was complete," partly on account of the fact that "the scientific Arnold brought forth the beauties of the immortal Handel."

For Paisiello the year 1787 was a good one, beginning in February with his comic opera *Il Tutor Burlato. Gli Schiavi Per Amore*, which opened on April 24, 1787 and was revived in 1788, enjoyed the longest run of all Italian operas during the years of this study with thirty performances, including five benefits. His *Il Re*

Teodoro a Venezia launched the 1787-1788 season on December 8th and received continued approval from *The Times* for its "refined, polished, and elegant" entertainment. The paper reiterated its pleasure in "some of the most scientific of . . . Paisiello's music" (February 18, 1788, p.3).

January, 1788 was a busy month at the King's Theater with the continued performances of the preceding operas, with revivals and with the opening on January 1st of Cimarosa's *La Locandiera*, of which *The Times* (January 17, 1788, p. 2) said: "the subject is truly operatical; and the piece, on the whole, bids fair to be as great a favourite with the Town as any we have seen for many years." The full column review acclaimed the performance, but the opera lasted only a month with seven productions.

The Lenten season opened on February 9th with *The Messiah*, and almost daily performances of various oratorios followed, including those that were traditionally performed weekly at Covent Garden and Drury Lane. The season for benefits was at hand, and dozens followed in quick succession. The Freemason Hall concerts as well as the Pantheon concerts continued to draw large audiences. The Gallini feuds swelled but with no disadvantage to the King's Theater, for the crowds continued to be pleased with the presentations of the operas already mentioned, and they anticipated the new one announced for March 4th — Storace's *La*

Cameriera Astuta. Cimarosa's *L'Olimpiade* first appeared on May 8th, with the notice that "its fame and the celebrity of Marchesi drew the fullest house that has been known this season, so much so that had there been fifty more boxes, they would have been taken" (May 9, 1788, p. 2).

As tradition dictated, the 1788-1789 opera season was to open in December after the meeting of Parliament, but another argument developed between Gallini and the Lord Chamberlain over the licensing problem, and the opening performance had to be postponed until after Christmas. Possibly to assuage disappointments following the delay or perhaps to whet appetites for the operatic delicacies to follow, an announcement of the entire cast assembled by Gallini for the coming year appeared in the paper on December 17th (p.1):

> The Manager respectfully informs the Nobility, Gentry and frequenters of the Opera that he has engaged the following Performers for the approaching season.

> ### SERIOUS OPERA
> Composer, Signor Tarchi
> Leader of the Band, Mr. Cramer
> First Soprano, Signor Luigi Marchesi
> First Tenor, Signor Giuseppe Borlevesi

Second Soprano, Signor Ballelli

Second Tenor, Signor Fineschi

Bass, Signor Torregiani

First Woman, Signora Giuliani

Second Woman, Madame Pieltain

COMIC OPERA

First Buffo Merro Carattere, Signor Borsilli

First Buffo Caricato, Signor Torregiani

Second Buffo Caricato, Signor Delicati

Second Buffo Merror Carattere, Signor Fineschi

First Buffa, Signora Delicati

Second Buffas, Signora Sestini and Signora Borsilli

Serious Woman, Signora Clementina Grariana

N.B. Signora Storace and Signor Benicci are
likewise engaged, but cannot make their
appearance before Easter.

First Ballet Master, Mons. Noverre

Second Ballet Master, Mons. Coinde

Principal Dancers

Mons. Didelot, Mons. Beaupre
Mademoiselle Adelaide, Mademoiselle Colombe
Mademoiselle Norman, Mademoiselle
De Chemin, Mademoiselle De Pain, &c, &c.[3]

After long delays, the season at last opened on January 10th with Martin y Soler's comic opera *Una Cosa Rara*. This was followed by *Ifigenia in Aulide* by Cherubini, "a very promising composer," as the newspaper observed (January 26, 1789, p.2). While its run was slightly marred by a riot on February 7th, of greater concern was a more serious battle heating up — this time between Gallini and *The Times*. Mingled with accusations and re-criminations, however, announcements for and reactions to Tarchi's *Il Disertore* and for Cimarosa's *La Villana Riconosciuta*, which ran for three nights in March "with but indifferent success," did appear. Of five performances of Gazzaniga's *La Vendemmia* in April the reporter noted: "not much can be said" (May 11, 1789, p.2). In June a catastrophic fire hit the King's Theatre, and performances were moved to Covent Garden, where operas of Piccini, Tarchi and Paisiello filled out the season well into July. In spite of the losses and difficulties resulting from the fire and the quarrels with Gallini, *The Times* coverage of operas continued to reflect enthusiasm and optimism.

It is clear from this study that the paper's "explorations" of musical activities were indeed ceaseless, as John Walter's statement of policy from the beginning had emphasized they should be. In addition to advertisements, announcements and green-room columns, innumerable essays, letters, reviews and observations concerning musical performances appeared regularly under such headings as "Musical Intelligence," "Theatre," "Opera," "Theatricals," and "Operaticals." Who the reporters were, who wrote under pseudonyms such as "A Ghost," "Peregrine Puff," "Vicarious," "Criticus," "Roscius," "Thespis" and "Harmonicus"— who the music reviewers were for the embryonic *Times* remains, for the most part, a mystery.

Reactions to what was seen and heard on the stage and reported by these observers, critics and columnists, from 1785 to 1789, were very similar in character to assessments and judgments by newspaper reporters of today. In fact, Charles B. Hogan observes: "By 1800 a pattern [of formal reviewing] had been established that has remained unaltered to this day."[4] Critics' appraisals, then as now, were highly varied in tone, ranging from caustic attacks and gratuitous advice to sensitive recognition of and praise for excellent performances. For example, one utterly unsympathetic columnist berated a hapless singer thus: "just because her hair was on fire gave her no reason to run off the stage screaming." Surely, there is a touch of irony in the compliment for Signora Benini, who sang "with fearlessness" and "was perfectly at home . . . from the lowest note to the top of her compass, which though not extraordinaire, is by judicious management made more of than Dame Nature perhaps ever intended" (January 11, 1787, p.2). But there can be no doubt of the complete candour of another critic's judgment of Signor Babbini's second performance in

Artaxerxes, which, he asserts, "confirms our opinion of his abilities," which have gone "from bad to worse, and is a strong illustration in the art of sinking" (April 22, 1785, p.2). Plainly the reporter who commended Signora Storace's performance in *Il Re Teodoro in Venezia* (Paisiello) had listened and responded with sensitivity: "her cantabile song in the first act . . . she sung *[sic]* with true pathos and expression . . . her obbligato *[sic]* song in the second act was executed in a stile of brilliancy and taste...."He applauded "the rapidity and articulation with which she executed the different arduous and masterly divisions" (December 17, 1787, p.3).

Most of the reviewers considered some or all of the following: the source of the opera, the story or fable if it were not a familiar one; distinctions in the music; the length of the opera — which sometimes seemed inordinately important; and the quality of the acting. While reporters noted that the fable of Paisiello's *Il Marchesi Tulipano* was drawn from "a story of John, Duke of Austria," and that Gresnich's *Alceste* was an abridgement from Metastasio, and while they cited sources for many additional operas, the major concerns of *The Times* accounts were, of course, the music and the musicians.

Music "lacking in grandeur and originality of composition" was deplored, but that abounding "with some of the flights of genius" or with "delicacy of turn and originality of stile" was commended. The reviewer of Gluck's and Metastio's *Alceste* observed: its music "partakes more of the uniform sweetness of Sacchini, than of the rich variety of Haydn." Its "peculiar excellence" is in the accompaniments, which "do not cover the voice . . . which is rarely the case," being "properly subservient, and by that means contribute powerfully to the grand effect" (December 25, 1786, p.2). Overtures were a frequent subject for praise, often for their "grandeur" or "boldness."

The composer received considerable attention in the reviews — an interest well illustrated in the following reaction to *La Cameriera Astuta* by Stephan Storace:

> The music bespeaks the hand of a master — the airs, which are happily diversified, have infinite merit in their several stiles *[sic]*. The Trios, Quartettes, and Finales have much ingenuity and intricacy of composition — the Finale to the first act is peculiarly grand and striking. Upon the whole, *La Cameriera Astuta* does great honour to Mr. Storace's genius, and ranks him among the first professors of the science.[5]

The critic does note some flaws in the work: "Several of the inferior airs should be omitted, — and the Recitative ought to be compressed. The opera is in its present state much too long . . ."

(March 5, 1788, p.3).

Excessive length of productions was seldom overlooked by the critics. The review of Tarchi's *Il Disertore* clearly demonstrated their concern: "Some disapprobation arose from the extreme length of the performance; it was near eleven before the curtain fell. [Most evening performances began at 7:30.] The last act in particular would derive considerable effect from the pruning knife . . . several of the airs allotted to the inferior personages might be dispensed with" (March 2, 1789, p.2). Even the "beauties of the immortal Handel" seem to have been enhanced by the brevity of the work, as one critic ended his review of *Giulio Cesare in Egitto*: "The opera is short and sweet — by a very little past ten the Coffee-room was crowded" (March 5, 1787, p.2).

The Londoners' regard for the acting abilities of the singers as well as for their vocal talents is readily apparent in the pages of *The Times*. The critical views that "good sense" might be expected from even the most meagre talent are reflected in this approbation of Morelli's role in *Il Re Teodoro*: "Morelli's acting seems wholly under the guidance of good sense; he despises the grimace and buffoonery so peculiar to the foreign school and which indeed predominates too much in our own" (December 17, 1787, p.3). In January there was more praise: "Morelli was as usual admirable! From having played the part so often, he is become more meliorated, and is now as much at ease as if the character were really his own" (January 7, 1788, p.2).

Even though writers for the green-room columns occasionally spoke with marked derision of such performers as Giuliano, Madame Mara, Rubinelli and Marchesi, audiences and critics were touched by the obvious magic of their voices when these operatic figures sang their favourite roles. If flaws were noticed, they were balanced with attention called to excellences. On one occasion, Giuliano's voice seemed to the reporter "extremely thin, and her upper notes to have a shrillness, at times rather grating than pleasing to the ear" (April 7, 1788, p.2), but another performance prompted the observation that "her recitatives are only excelled by Marchesi" (February 2, 1789, p.2). Columnists praised Rubinelli's "richness of tones" and "wonderful powers" and the "magnificence of (Anna) Storace and Morelli" and declared the voice of Marchesi to be a "tower of strength." Reporters were moved by Mara's "delicacy and feeling," which, when she was at her best, were "exquisitely characteristic and pleasing."

Italian opera was performed for sophisticated and knowledgeable audiences, and the various columns of *The Times* mirrored the taste and temper of that public as well as that of the critics. If the opera were to satisfy the Londoner, it must not be — in the words of the reporters — "dull" or "flat" or "unprofitable." It would please if it reflected "pathos and expression," "science," "good humour," "spirit," "taste," and "vivacity." If the performer were to earn the plaudits of the London audience, he must combine "excellence of voice, taste, execution, expression, and action."

From this study of *The Times* (1785-1789), it is obvious that the interest and enthusiasm for Italian opera shown by the London audience was impressive. Thirty different operas were on the boards from January 1, 1785 until December 31, 1789. Eighteen composers were represented in this period — Paisiello, Cimarosa and Tarchi were the most frequently performed. *Gli Schiavi Per Amore, L'Olimpiade* and *Virginia* held the stage for the longest runs. Altogether, there were over two hundred twenty-five operatic presentations. Since, in the entire first year of *The Times* (1785) only a single opera was reported, the total number of performances announced in these years is all the more striking.

The King's Theater, colorful in its long and turbulent history, subject to bickerings and quarrels over the years, made available to the London public the best operas and performers from the continent. Composers of international repute and illustrious singers were highly acclaimed by the *cognoscenti*. Many of these artists remained in England for long periods of time, and their energetic involvement in the musical activities of London as well as those of other cities in England is a matter of record in the daily columns of *The Times*. A relatively new addition to the newspaper organization, the reporters or reviewers of music activities, while lacking the distinction of the literary style of later music critics, were interested in communicating a straightforward appraisal of what they saw and heard, expressing plainly their likes and dislikes, based upon their experience and observation. Their accounts provide a richly revealing picture of the role of Italian opera in the London scene from 1785 to 1789. Italian opera had indeed found "a generous advocate" in *The Times* — as John Walter had promised his early readers the paper would be.

FOOTNOTES

[1]For clarity and brevity, all references to the *Daily Universal Register* (D. U. R.) and to *The Times* (the new name given the paper on 17th March, 1788) will be placed in the text following or near the quotation. Occasional inconsistencies in the spelling of singers' names or in the titles of operas appear in the newspaper.

[2]Charles Burney, *A General History of Music from the Earliest Ages to the Present Period (1789)*, new edition with Critical and Historical Notes by Frank Mercer (2 vols.; London: Foulis; New York: Harcourt, 1935; New York: Dover Publications, 1957), 11, p.897.

[3]The following additional data concerning subscribers, reservations and tickets were included in this notice:

> Those subscribers of last season, who have not yet signified their intention, respecting the retaining of their boxes, are respectfully requested to send their names in writing by Saturday next, to the Treasurer's Office, in Union Court, Haymarket, or the Manager will be under the necessity of disposing of their Boxes. All persons claiming admission into the Opera-House by Silver Tickets, or Renters' Shares are requested to send the same to the Treasurer's Office, as early as may be, that they may be examined, and properly certified, otherwise they cannot be admitted (17th December, 1788, p.1).

[4]Charles Beecher Hogan, *The London Stage, 1776-1800: A Critical Introduction* (Carbondale, Illinois: Southern Illinois University Press, 1968), p. clxxviii.

[5]Storace and his sister Anna, while English by birth, were of Italian descent and received music training in Italy. Anna was greatly admired on the continent and in England as a soloist.

The London Music Scene
1785-1789, as Reflected in *The Times*

While the musical scene of late 18th-century London has been characterized sometimes as undistinguished, evidence found in a study of *The Times,* 1785-1789, does indicate that the surprising variety and vast quantity of music made available to the public, and the energetic support given by large and enthusiastic audiences, generated a musical vigor and vitality many another period might envy. The latter quarter of the century in England was distinguished by such musical figures as J. C. Bach and K. F. Abel, by Muzio Clementi, the Cramers — father and son, by Dr. Arne and Dr. Arnold, by William Shield, violinist, composer, and friend of Haydn, and by the impressario, Johann Peter Salomon. Moreover, this was the world into which, following Salomon's successful coup in arranging for his visit, the great Haydn moved in January 1791. The "large, excellently trained orchestras" at his disposal were, according to Geiringer, a deciding factor in Haydn's decision to come to England.[1] The composers and instrumentalists helped to create the climate in which an era of astonishing activity in orchestral performance in this country was to be opened.

Musical theatre, opera, and choral performances were all major attractions in the London scene at this time and were abundantly covered by the newspapers. Variously announced in *The Times* as comic operas, musical comedies, pastoral operas, burlettas, pasticcios, and adaptations, the English operas were produced in endless succession at Covent Garden, Drury Lane, and the Haymarket. In the first six months of 1785, more than one hundred twenty-five performances of these plays were presented at these three theaters. That Italian Opera in London was a flourishing enterprise is reflected in *The Times* record of more than two hundred twenty-five presentations from 1785-1789. Large-scale vocal and choral works, presented almost weekly, attracted widespread interest. The oratorio, long revered in the great city, was probably, of all musical activities, the most eagerly awaited. Accompaniments for these works were played by "the band," made up of eminent instrumentalists, who further enhanced these performances with overtures or concertos or instrumental solos between the acts and between the choral numbers.

But it was the concert room, public and private, that gave the instrumentalists their major avenues for artistic achievement and provided the London musical scene with another highly significant dimension. Subscription concerts had enjoyed a tradition dating from the early part of the century and were flourishing during the latter half of the 1780's. The most famous of these were the Professional Concerts at Hanover Square, Salomon's Concerts,[2] Mara's Concerts, the Pantheon Concerts, and the Freemason Hall Subscriptions. A second major category of concerts was provided by the music membership societies, the most prestigious of which were the Academy of Antient Music, the Concert of Ancient Music, and the more convivial but none-the-less serious, Anacreontic Society. In addition to these important subscription series and membership society concerts, other public concerts at the famous pleasure gardens Vauxhall and Ranelagh attracted throngs of people during the summer months. Spliced into the busy schedules of these musical activities were dozens of "benefits" for individual artists and for charities. Further, numerous private concerts, called "morning concerts" or "Sunday evening concerts" or "ladies concerts," were provided by the wealthy in the great houses.

Those events, seen burgeoning in a variety of settings and formats, prompted increasing numbers of notices and appraisals by newspapers and journals. Of particular note are the illuminating insights into the musical taste and practices of the period presented by the newly established *Times* (1785), first called *The Daily Universal Register*. Through its daily columns, the essential character of the London music scene, 1785-1789, becomes plainly apparent, and the newspaper's accounts make abundantly clear London's increasing interest in the "concert."

Largest and most prestigious of the subscription series, the Professional Concerts were given at the Hanover Square Rooms. This particular series was the ultimate fruit of the weekly programs which were initiated in 1764 by Karl Friedrich Abel and Johann Christian Bach, who came from Germany in 1759 and 1762. On February 1, 1775 these two musicians opened the new Hanover Square Rooms with a joint recital. These recitals continued there until Bach's death in 1782. In 1783, a few instrumentalists led by Wilhelm Cramer joined together, to give "professional" concerts at this location.[3] But it was not until February 2, 1785, as W. T. Parke noted in his *Memoirs,* that the Hanover Square Concerts for the first time presented its program under the name Professional Concerts.[4]

Several aspects of the programs, which were offered from early February through April, are particularly noteworthy: the predominance of instrumental music and the choice of composers represented in the music selected. Overtures, symphonies, concertos, divertementi, quintettos by such popular composers as Bach, Abel, Clementi,Handel, Mozart, and Pleyel were frequently heard. The chief interest was in contemporary music. In the ten programs published by *The Times,* works by the greatly admired Haydn appeared eight times, twice on the February 2, 1789 concert. The list of performers for the 1787 season of the Professional Concerts (*The Times,* January 24) including thirty-three instrumentalists, "composer, Mr. Abel" and "Leader of the Band, Mr. Cramer," and three singers, illustrates the structure of the full orchestra and the quality of its musicians.

A second impressive subscription series was launched at the Pantheon in 1787 by Mme. Gertrude Elisabeth Schmeling Mara, whose extraordinary musical abilities and charm attracted attention at home and abroad. Though she was the leading soprano of the period, Mara's concerts emphasized instrumental rather than vocal music. She placed twenty-eight concertos on the ten 1788 programs published by *The Times:* ten for hautboy were played by Fischer; seven for French horn, by Ponto; six for violin, by Raimondi. For four flute concertos Graff was the soloist, and for one concerto, Mons. Mara was the principal instrumentalist. In addition to the concertos, there were eleven "overtures,"[5] seven of which were by Haydn, and ten pieces for ensemble: two quintets, one trio, and six quartettos, one of these by Haydn for "two violins, tenor, and violoncello."

Another major subscription series at the Pantheon, given in the magnificent Rotunda, bore the name of the hall itself. The structure of the eleven programs studied followed in general the prevailing pattern of a first and second act, the first number of each act being a "full piece." A particular distinction in the Pantheon Concerts was the invariable inclusion of a "glee" in the first act and a "catch" in the second, most frequently drawn from Purcell or Arne. The presence of these pieces, while balancing almost evenly the vocal and instrumental works, lengthened the programs to as many as fifteen numbers! (Mara's programs ran to nine or ten; the

Professional Concerts, usually eleven.) Haydn and Abel, the most frequently programmed composers, were each played six times, Corelli four, and Stamitz three. While concertos were not so frequent as in the other subscription concerts, on these eleven programs there were ten for violin and six concertos or "duettos" for French horn played by the Leander brothers.

The Freemasons Hall was the locale for still another important subscription series. Opened in May 1776, this building, designed for the purposes of the Freemasons' organization, was the setting for many concerts and benefits. The Freemasons Hall Subscription series, unusual because it combined literary readings and music, was initiated in August 1786. A September 27th announcement in *The Times* indicated ambitious programs to come. The subscriptions were to be limited to three hundred members, and the admission for each subscriber was to be one guinea. Among the literary figures represented were Milton, Dryden,, Richardson, Swift, Thomson, Fielding, Pope, Young, Sterne, Garrick, and Sheridan.

The nine programs printed in *The Times,* 1785-1789, indicate that the musical portions of these composite concerts were in many ways similar to the programs of the other subscriptions. "Overtures" were chosen from Arne, Gluck, and Haydn. In four out of the nine presentations, the concluding number was a "Grand

Overture" by Haydn — indeed, on December 16, 1786, the finale to the first act as well as that to the second was a Haydn "Grand Overture." Concertos were especially popular with this series, being represented, in addition to Haydn, by Handel, Corelli, Avison, Hoffman, Pleyel, and Giornovichi.

Rivalling the professional concerts in importance were the musical activities of the prestigious membership societies: the Academy of Antient Music, Concerts of Ancient Music, and the Anacreontic Society. The oldest of these was the Academy established in 1726. Its earliest director was Dr. Pepusch. Traditionally, the society met fortnightly with various members planning the concerts, a custom also followed by the two other membership organizations.

The Academy's interest, during the period 1785-1789, seems to have been divided between vocal and instrumental music. Much of the music in their programs was drawn from the earlier composers Byrd, Pergolesi, and Handel, but contemporary composers were often heard. Dr. Arne was a great favorite.

The Times accounts of these concerts were usually generous in length, generally mild, and quite respectful. The audience for the December 18, 1789 opening of the winter season was declared to be "brilliant and fashionable." The selection of pieces for this particular evening was made by the Duke of Leeds. Dr. Arnold, the director from 1789-1792, was at the organ, and Salomon was the leader of the band, both (*The Times* said) "most excellent in their departments." According to the newspaper's estimate, the number of members and guests attending these concerts ranged from three hundred to as many as seven hundred.

A second influential society, the Concerts of Ancient Music, was organized in 1776 and continued through mid-nineteenth century. Directed by a number of noblemen, the Concert's standing was enhanced in 1785 when the king and the royal family gave their support to the programs by their attendance --- whence the additional title, King's Concerts. The meetings were held in rooms built in 1772 by Francis Pasquali and subsequently known as Pasquali's Rooms.[6] Here, interested audiences gathered to listen to music by "venerable composers" such as Purcell, Corelli, Gluck, Pergolesi, and Handel. An oddity in programming resulted from the society's policy which required that the music, selected by one of its members, should have been composed at least twenty years earlier — a practice accounting undoubtedly for the absence of Haydn's name from its programs. From *The Times* critics, who continually demonstrated their greater interest in contemporary music, notices were infrequent and brief; critical reactions were often indifferent and occasionally caustic.

For the productions of the third membership organization, the Anacreontic Society, *The Times* commendation was unequivocal. In the January 8, 1785 issue of the new *Daily Universal Register,* a third of a column was devoted to a report of the "Anacreontic Meeting." The article concluded: "In short, it must be said that for elegance of company, joined to elegance of music and song, the Anacreontic takes the lead of all other musical meetings in Europe." A little excessive, perhaps, but close study of the society's activities, as they are subsequently described in *The Times,* indicates the excellence of the music selected and the high quality of the performances. W. T. Parke, who became a member in 1786, characterized the performers as "the flower of the musical profession." Founded in 1766, this fashionable society limited its membership, but members were privileged to introduce friends. Meetings were held fortnightly in the great ballroom of the Crown and Anchor Tavern (home of the Academy of Antient Music in its earlier days). Assemblies were large, *The Times* reporting upon occasion, audiences "near four hundred strong." Non-concert activities, including catches, glees, songs, toasts, the traditional singing of the Anacreontic Hymn, and a good supper probably added to the attractions of the meetings, but seem not to have detracted from the seriousness of the Society's attention to the music of both the old masters and the new.

The Anacreontic programs, as *The Times* excellent coverage demonstrated, differed somewhat from the concerts of the various subscriptions series and from those of the other membership societies. Emphasis was steadily placed upon contemporary music. A typical program consisted of two or three "overtures" or symphonies, several concertos, and one or two instrumental ensembles. Pleyel's quartettos and Clementi's pianoforte sonatas were popular. The two most significant contemporary composers represented were Haydn and Mozart. In *The Times* reviews studied, Haydn's name appears most often. Many of the concerts began with one of his "overtures" or closed with one of his "grand symphonies." Mozart's music was frequently on the Anacreontic programs, most often for the 1787 and 1788 meetings. The third concert in this season (November 7, 1787) opened and closed with his symphonies. On November 14, 1788, *The Times* reported a recent program which included his "new trio for the Pianoforte, Violin, and Tenor . . . admirably performed by Messrs. Clementi, Cramer, and Blake."

In a distinctively different setting, the public concerts taking place in the famous pleasure gardens of Ranelagh and Vauxhall during the summer months drew great crowds of people from all classes of society. Here, music competed with fireworks, exhibitions, picnics, promenades, regattas, masquerades, and ridottos, and audiences assembled to hear professional performances of Haydn, Handel, Geminiani, Bach, and Paiesiello. Ranelagh began to decline in "fashion" and "in the quality of its music" during the early 70's, as *The Times* slim coverage of the gardens' activities in the latter half of the 1780's reflects.

In contrast, Vauxhall was highly fashionable during this later period, and its music activities were flourishing. Hook was the director, organist, and composer for these programs, which were regularly published in *The Times*. Leading instrumental soloists in the popular concertos were Parke, Pieltain, Parkinson, and the Leander brothers. On the fifty-nine programs for the summers of 1786 and 1787 printed in *The Times,* Haydn was again the most popular composer, performed in thirty-three out of thirly-five concerts in 1786 and twenty-two out of twenty-four in 1787. Handel's music held its own with fifty-five appearances on fifty-nine programs, and Bach's work was heard on twenty-nine programs. Abel, Arne, Richter, and Stamitz were frequently programmed.

Innumerable benefit concerts for musicians as well as for charities were fitted into the teeming schedule of London music activities which always accelerated after the turn of the year. On the whole, these concerts followed the usual program structure of two acts, an instrumental piece to open and close the program, with vocal and instrumental music alternating. Orchestral music abounded. It is no surprise to find Haydn's music the most frequently played—on thirty-five out of fifty programs examined. For

31

the benefits, the concerto was a major item—more than a hundred in *The Times* accounts. Violinists and oboists were most in demand as soloists, but at least fifteen pianoforte concertos were played.

Private concerts were still another distinctive musical activity regularly reported in *The Times* during the 1785-1789 period. The royal family and the nobility frequently attended these programs in the great houses. Many members of these households were themselves good amateur instrumentalists and often performed as soloists or with professionals for their friends and guests. Upon his first visit to London, Haydn referred in several letters to this interest in performance which he had observed. He described   visits to the country seat of the Duke of York where he heard the Duchess play the pianoforte, and where on another occasion he and the Prince of Wales played music "for 4 hours in the evening...."

Clearly, the reporters for *The London Times* followed with avid interest the numerous Subscription and Society programs, and the many public and private concerts which were being performed in the various Rooms, Halls, Gardens, and great houses. From this study of the newspaper accounts of the instrumental programs during the years 1785-1789, it is evident that symphonies, "overtures," and concertos were the most popular forms of instrumental music, and further, that there was considerable interest in ensemble and chamber music: duettos, trios, quartettos, and quintets for various combinations of instruments. With excellent music composed for it, the pianoforte was rapidly growing in popularity, being often heard in concertos, in solo performances, and as an accompanying instrument. Among the distinguished instrumentalists most often cited and commended in *The Times* were: Karl Friedrich Abel, the great viola da gambist; Parke and Fischer, the eminent oboists; French horn players Ponto, Pieltain, and the "unrivalled" Leander brothers; clarinetist Mahon, and flutists Potter and Decamp, Serjeant, who played the trumpet; and the "Herculean" Gariboldi, who astonished his hearers with the "thunder" of his double bass; Muzio Clementi recognized as the preeminent harpsichordist, pianofortist, and teacher of the day and his gifted pupil Johann Baptist Cramer. Wilhelm Cramer, "consummate master of his art," and Johann Peter Salomon, "long at the very top of his profession," were the premier violinists of the period.

A careful reading of *The London Times,* 1785-1789, reveals audiences, large, informed, lively, and actively interested in instrumental music; abundant music, old and new, readily accessible; and performers, gifted, accomplished, and busy in their professional engagements. Much of the music and many of the performers continue to occupy significant places in music history. Further, close examination of the newspaper shows that instrumental performances --- subscription series, membership-society programs, summer park concerts, benefits, and a host of private musicales --- were indeed competing successfully for their share of the musical audience in a London scene crowded with musical theater, with opera and oratorio.

In his *Musical Memoirs*, W. T. Parke noted that by 1784 instrumental music in London had "arrived at a high degree of perfection."[4] The activities of the subsequent five years (1785-1789) as revealed in the illuminating columns of *The London Times* fully justify Parke's tribute to his fellow musicians. London was indeed ready to welcome Haydn one year hence.

FOOTNOTES

[1]Karl Geiringer, *Haydn* (Berkeley and Los Angeles: University of California Press, 1968), p. 101.

[2]Johann Peter Salomon, renowned violinist and member of the Professional Concerts, removed himself from that group in 1784 and formed his own in 1786. It was he who succeeded in bringing Haydn to England, and it was for the Salomon's Concerts that Haydn composed the twelve London symphonies. While *The Times* consistently praised Salomon's artistry as a soloist, as an instrumentalist in small ensembles and larger orchestras, and as a conductor, his Concerts received almost no notice by this paper during this five-year period.

[3]This chapter in London's music history is treated in detail in Charles Sanford Terry's *John Christian Bach* (2nd edition; London, New York, Toronto: Oxford University Press, 1967), pp. 141-169.

[4]W.T. Parke, *Musical Memoirs* (London: Henry Colburn and Richard Bentley, 1830; reprint, New York: Da Capo Press, 1970), I, 53.

[5]Distinctions between the terms "overture," "symphony," "full piece," "grand overture," "divertemente," and the like, as they appeared on the programs in the newspapers, are not always clear

[6]See Robert Elkins' *The Old Concert Rooms of London* (London: Edward Arnold, 1955), pp. 65-71, for an excellent history and description of this hall.

[7]William Sandys and Simon Andrew Forster, *The History of the Violin* (London: William Reeves, 1864), p. 177. According to Sandys and Forster, the actual size of the 1789 Academy of Antient Music band and the distributions of the parts were "1 organ, 14 violins, Barthelemon being the first, 4 violas, 4 violoncellos, 3 hautboys, 2 trumpets, 2 horns, 3 bassoons, 2 double bassoons, and 1 drum."

[8]For further details concerning these rooms, see Elkins, pp. 82-91.

[9]Parke, I, 81.

[10]"The Star-Spangled Banner" was set to this tune which was composed by John Stafford Smith, 1750-1836.

[11]Mollie Sands' *Invitation to Ranelagh, 1742-1803* (London: John Westhouse, 1947) provides a colorful account of the activities of this pleasure garden. Illustrious guests at Ranelagh included Mozart, who at the age of eight played the harpsichord and organ there, and twenty-eight years later his friend, Joseph Haydn, who attended a benefit there. Sands, pp. 91-92 and pp. 183-184. See also Terry, pp. 79-80 and Robbins Landon, The *Collected Correspondence and Notebooks of Joseph Haydn* (London: Barrie and Rockliff; 1959), pp. 257-258.

[12]Landon, p. 123.

[13]Parke, I, 36.

Karl Friedrich Abel
Some Contemporary Impressions

To Karl Friedrich Abel, the great viola da gamba virtuoso and composer and long-time resident in London until his death in 1787, is probably due much of the credit for maintaining interest in the viola da gamba as a principal solo instrument and as a member of ensembles in England until the latter part of the eighteenth century. The decline in the popularity of this last survivor of the viol family, foreshadowed by the 1750's, may be attributed in some measure to contemporary response to the tonal character of the instrument itself. Thomas Busby, music historian, complained that the "thin" and "wiry" tones were difficult to "render attractive" and scarcely to be endured,[1] and Charles Burney noted that the "greatest skill and refinement" were required to make the instrument's tones "bearable."[2] Such "skill and refinement" were united in the person of Abel, whose dedication and genius brought the long colorful history of the instrument to a splendid close.

Abel, born in Cothen in 1723, arrived in London in 1759, and with his high degree of musical competence augmented the already vigorous artistic life of the city. Blessed with early tutelage from his father and Johann Sebastian Bach in Leipzig and equipped with extensive experience gained in various musical centers in Germany, he quickly established himself in his new abode as a musician of unusual skill with particular fame as a player of the viola da gamba. He was soon appointed chamber musician to Queen Charlotte. At various times he was principal composer for numerous musical organizations in the city, including the Hanover Square Professional Concerts which was founded in 1785. His close friend Johann Christian Bach arrived in London in the fall of 1762, and on January 23, 1763, the two instrumentalists gave the first of their joint concerts, a series which continued until Bach's death in 1783. After the loss of his friend, Abel returned to Germany where he remained for two years, but by January 1785, he was again in London.

January 1785 was significant not only for Abel's return to the British concert halls, but also for the launching of the new and powerful newspaper, *The Daily Universal Register* (later called *The Times*), its initial edition appearing on January 1. Consistently an ardent supporter of musical activities in the city, this young and energetic daily paper carried for the first time on January 11 a column entitled "Musical Intelligence." In this account of musical activities is found the first of many references to Abel made by *The Times* — references found in announcements of programs and concerts, reviews of performances, and in green-room gossip columns. The announcement of the program "lately held at the Duke of Queensberry's" was typically lacking in distinctions between composer and performer and sparse in particularity of detail.

"Eminent professors" presented this private concert which was as follows:

> Concerto, violin, Mr. Lolli
> Concerto, viol de gambo, Mr. Abel
> Concerto, harpsichord, Mr. Schroeter
> Concerto, violin, Mr. Cramer
> Concerto, violin, Mr. Salomon
> Concerto, oboe, Mr. Parke
> Quartetto, in which Mr. Salomon led
> Solo, on the violin, Mr. Lolli
> Overture .[3]

No review of this presentation was printed, but in the following week the "Musical Intelligence" carried an account of the "grand concert at Lord Brudenell's at which were present his Royal Highness the Prince of Wales, the foreign Ambassadors, and many of the nobility." The reviewer wrote on January 17, 1785, p.3: "Abel was perfection."[4]

This reaction to Abel's performance is typical of the high esteem in which his extraordinary ability was held. Other contemporary sources support this regard. W. T. Parke, the eminent oboist, paid frequent tribute to Abel in his *Memoirs*, commending his inimitable performance.[5] Parke, recalling Abel's playing for the first

Professional Concert at Hanover Square on February 2, 1785, noted that he "performed a solo on the viol di gamba with his accustomed elegance and sensibility."[6] Gerber spoke of "the greatness of his talent, his wonderful power of expression, the richness of his tones, and his stirring execution on the gamba."[7] In its tribute upon Abel's death in 1787, *The London Chronicle*, June 30, 1787, declared his "great musical ability . . . an honour to the age in which he lived" and observed: "As to the Viol di Gamba, the instrument is now lost."[8]

Abel's command of his instrument was described as having been distinguished by several characteristics which regularly caught the attention of his hearers: his "hand" which "no difficulties could embarrass," his taste which was "most refined and delicate," his judgment "so correct and certain as never to let a single note escape without meaning."[9] The critic for the *Gentleman's Magazine* thought that "no person ever touched that instrument with sweeter effect or taste,"[10] and Busby recalled Abel's "always pleasing and frequently learned modulation"[11] —presumably modulation of tone in expressive phrasing. "His taste and knowledge," Gerber said, "especially made him the umpire on all contested points .... "[12] Abel's particular excellence in playing an adagio frequently elicited such comments as these made by Gerber: "On his first appearance in London, his discretion, his taste, and his pathetic manner of expression in the rendering of his adagios so captivated the young virtuosi that they very soon followed his school with less expenditure of notes and with more successful result."[13] Burney, equally impressed, wrote: " . . . in nothing was he so superior to himself, and to other musicians, as in writing and playing an *adagio*; in which the most pleasing, yet learned modulation; the richest harmony; and the most elegant and polished melody were all expressed with such feeling, taste, and science, that no musical production or performance with which I was then [1779] acquainted seemed to approach nearer perfection."[14] The writer for the *European Magazine*, May, 1784, assessing his performing abilities as "truly excellent," was convinced that "no modern has been heard to play an *adagio* with greater taste and feeling than Mr. Abel."[15]

At a time when the popularity of solo instrumental and orchestral music was reaching new heights, opportunities for hearing music in London by such eminent composers as Haydn, Mozart, Bach, Stamitz, and Clementi were many. From a study of programs presented throughout the city and a review of the critics' reactions, it is apparent that Abel's niche as a composer for the gamba and as a modern symphonist was as assured as was his position as an instrumentalist in the London music scene. Indicative of his appeal as a composer is the frequency with which his music appeared on programs printed in *The Times* from 1785 until his death in May, 1787. During this relatively brief period, his music was performed on no fewer than twenty-four occasions. Many concerts began with an Abel "Full Piece" — probably an entire symphony, although in journalistic writing of the day, musical terms such as symphony and overture and full piece sometimes were inconsistently applied. Hanover Square Professional Concerts frequently opened their first or second "act" with a "Symphony" or an "Overture" of his.

Critics almost without exception praised Abel's compositions. His overtures, quartets, concertantes, and symphonies were acclaimed for their originality, richness of style, their beauty and grandeur. A *Times* columnist, writing on June 23 shortly after Abel's death, noted that "Sensibility is the prevailing and beautiful characteristic of his compositions." One writer for *The London Chronicle* on October 12, 1787 recalled that Abel's "forte was the pathetic" and commended the "rich vein of melody [which] runs through all his *andante* movements."[16] Earlier, another reporter for the same paper had called attention to "the subjects of his movements, and the elegant combinations of his harmony...."[17] The *Edinburgh Magazine* and *Literary Miscellany* reflected similar praise, adding that his genius "must ever be attended with admiration."[18] Almost a decade after Abel's death, the *Monthly Magazine* and *British Register* reminded its readers that Abel's works abounded "with expression, with fine and pleasing (though sometimes abstruse) modulation, and with accuracy of composition."[19] Burney particularly commended Abel's "musical science in harmony, modulation, fugue, and canon .... " Of his last quartets, Burney remarked that they constituted a "specimen of his science and care in the composition and arrangement of the parts ... [which were] in point of harmony and selection of sounds, models of perfection .... " Abel's compositions, he said, were "easy and elegantly simple." Abel's own words seem to suggest a key to this musical desideratum: "I do not chuse to be always struggling with difficulties, and playing with all my might."[20]

Some critics did, however, question the spirit and vitality of Abel's work. According to the writer for the *European Magazine*, who noted "a uniformity . . . through all his works," Abel's "sweet and flowing" music was "seldom spirited and great."[21] Even Burney could observe: "As his invention was not unbounded, and his exquisite taste and deep science prevented the admission of whatever was not highly polished, there seemed in some of his last productions a languor and monotony .... "[22]

Abel's patrons and friends included members of the royalty and nobility, musicians, composers, journalists, historians, dramatists, and artists. One of his most valued friendships was with Thomas Gainsborough who painted two portraits of his friend, one of which hangs in the Huntington Library in California.[23] While Gainsborough's profession was painting, he had a life-long passion for music, and, according to William Jackson of Exeter, "flirted with" many instruments including the hautboy and violin, but each visit with Abel "brought him back to the viola da gamba."[24] Abel's apartment walls were covered with Gainsborough's pictures, an "exchange for the notes of his *viol-di-gamba*," as Henry Angelo recorded in his *Reminiscences*. A "tall, portly person" with a "dry humour," according to Angelo, Abel seems to have been warmly regarded by all who knew him.[25] Sainsbury recalled that Abel "kept on tolerable terms with society, though a natural irascibility and disposition to say strong things, sometimes rendered him overbearing and insolent in company."[26] Even so, while he was known to lose his temper when pressed, he was admired for his affability and generosity. William Jackson called him "the prince of musicians." When Abel died, his friend Gainsborough wrote eloquently to Henry Bate: "We love a genius for what he leaves and we mourn him for what he takes away ... For my part, I shall never cease looking up to heaven ... in hopes of getting one more glance of the man I loved from the moment I heard him touch the string ... "[27]

FOOTNOTES

[1]Thomas Busby, *A General History of Music from the Earliest Time to the Present*, Comprising the Lives of Eminent Composers and Musical Writers (2 vols.; London: Printed for G. and W. B. Whittaker, Ave-Maria Lane and Simpkin and Marshall, Stationers' Court, 1819; New York: Da Capo Press, 1968), 11, 517.

[2]Charles Burney, *A General History of Music from the Earliest Ages to the Present Period* (1789), new edition with Critical and Historical Notes by Frank Mercer (2 vols.; London: Foulis; New York: Harcourt. 1935; New York: Dover Publications, 1957), 11, 1020.

[3]*Daily Universal Register* (later *The Times*), January 11, 1785; p. 3, c.

[4]*The Times*, January 17, 1785; p. 3. c. 4.

[5]W. T. Parke *Musical Memoirs* (London: Henry Colburn and Richard Bentley, 1830), I, 62.

[6]*Ibid.,* I, 53.

[7]Ernst Ludwig Gerber, quoted by Wilhelm Joseph von Wasielewski, *The Violoncello and Its History* (London and New York: Novello, Ewer and Co., 1894; New York: Da Capo Press, 1968), p. 33.

[8]*London Chronicle*, June 30, 1787; p.3, c.3.

[9]Burney, II, 1019.

[10]*Gentleman's Magazine.* 57 (1787), Pt. 1, p. 549.

[11]Busby, II, 517.

[12]Gerber, quoted by Wasielewski, p. 33.

[13] *Ibid.,* pp, 32-33.

[14]Burney, 11, 1019.

[15]*European .Magazine*, May 1784, p. 366.

[16]*London Chronicle*, October 12, 1787; p. 356, c.3.

[17]*Ibid.,* June 21, 1787; p. 592, c. 3

[18]*Edinburgh Magazine and Literary Miscellany*, June 1787, p. 311.

[19]*Monthly Magazine* and *British Register*, December 1796 (Supplement) pp. 981-986.

[20]Burney, II, 1019-1020.

[21]*European Magazine*, May 1784, p. 366.

[22]Burney, II, 1020.

[23]The informal portrait painted by the French artist, Charles Jean Robineau, is in sharp contrast to Gainsborough's which shows Abel in powdered wig and formal court dress with his viola da gamba.

[24]William Jackson, *The Four Ages, Together with Essays on Various Subjects* (London: Printed for Cadell and Davies, 1798; New York, Garland Publishing, Inc., 1970), pp. 148-151.

[25]Henry Angelo, *The Reminiscences of Henry Angelo* (London: Henry Colburn and Richard Bentley, 1830; 2 vols.; New York: Benjamin Blom, 1969), I, passim.

[26]John Sainsbury, A *Dictionary of Musicians From the Earliest Times* (2 vols.; London: n.p., 1825; New York: Da Capo Press, 1966), I,2.

[27]From a letter written June 20, 1787. Mary Woodall, *The Letters of Thomas Gainsborough* (London: Lion and Unicorn Press at the Royal College of Art, 1961; Greenwich, Connecticut: New York Graphic Society, 1963), p. 31.

The Critic and Stage Music
The London Music Scene
1785-1794

The music scene in late 18th-century London was distinguished by vigorous activity from its composers and performers, and by enthusiastic support of theater audiences, coinciding with increased reports and appraisals from journalists. Music historians generally agree that artistic achievements of real and lasting value were relatively slight; yet a detailed, widely ranging, and colorful record of London's musical achievements can be found in the pages of *The London Times*, newly established on January 1, 1785. Called *The Daily Universal Register* until its name was changed in 1788, the young and enterprising newspaper gave to its public (and posterity) a vigorous and fresh accounting of — as its founder, John Walter, promised on January 2, 1786 — "the Italian Opera, Oratorio, every concert and other Musical Meeting of Reputation." A study of the paper from 1785-1789 provides, then, a rich sampling of the expanding musical scene in London in the latter half of the 1780's.

During this period, an abundance of musical activity (instrumental concerts, vocal and choral performances, and stage music) continuously attracted large numbers of the ever-increasing entertainment-conscious public. If one's interests were in instrumental as well as vocal music, the subscription concerts provided such choices as the Concert of Ancient Music programs, which had prospered as a joint interest of Karl Friedrich Abel and Johann Christian Bach. Conservative in its programming, this series continued to provide the public with "old music." The Professional Concerts catered, for the most part, to the more "contemporary" tastes and not only provided opportunities for new music to be heard, but brought before the public — in addition to English performers — renowned singers from the continent whose residence in London prompted increased activity. Such concert halls as Hanover Square Rooms, Tottenham Street Rooms, Hickford Rooms, Haberdasher's Hall, and Freemasons' Hall were the settings for these concerts and for "benefits" which, particularly in the spring, appeared in rapid succession and gave more opportunities for favorite performers to be heard.

Vocal or choral works on a large scale were presented almost weekly. The frequency of the reporting by *The Times* suggests that, of all musical events, the oratorio was probably the most eagerly awaited. The distinguished 1784 Handel Commemoration was by no means an isolated occurrence, for the presentation of Handel's works, which, not on so large a scale as the 1784 Westminster performance, could be expected for any musically important occasion, as the numerous notices in *The Times* demonstrate. The Lenten season prompted the traditional oratorio performances at Covent Garden, Drury Lane, and Tottenham Street Rooms.

Interest in Italian opera had long been a strong tradition in the great City. The reporting of more than two hundred and twenty-five presentations of Italian opera by *The Times*, 1785-1789, indicates the great enthusiasm on the part of the music public for such illustrious singers as Madame Mara, Ferrarese, Rubinelli, and Marchesi as they sang the leading roles in the operas of Italian composers Sacchini, Paisiello, Cimarosa, Tarchi, 'and others of equal repute.

All of these forms of entertainment were continuously noted in the daily columns of *The Times*, but the most popular attractions were to be found in the theaters in the form of stage music, the prolific production of which was fed by the very nature of the London theater itself. Only two theaters in London, Covent Garden and Drury Lane, were "patented" or "chartered" to produce legitimate drama, that is, drama without music. This monopoly, the control of which was in the hands of the Lord Chamberlain, had been established in 1660 by Charles II and continued to be held by these two major theaters until the middle of the nine-teenth century.[1] Unable, within the law, to present plays except under the masquerade of music, the minor theaters such as Astley's, Royal Grove, Royal Circus, Sadler's Wells, and Royalty Theater, produced plays or drama to which, of necessity, music had to be added, the result being a spate of effusions called musical farces, pantomimes, burlettas, pasticcios, comic operas (the most popular form), and the like. The patented or major theaters (i.e., Drury Lane and Covent Garden), on the other hand, hindered by none of the disadvantages which encumbered the lesser theaters, were perfectly free to borrow from these theaters ideas and practices which had proved to be popular and profitable. The range of these miscellaneous musical entertainments as announced and categorized in *The Daily Universal Register* can be seen in the following sampling: *Harmonic Jubilee* was called a "musical interlude;" *Arthur and Emmiline* was a "masque with vocal parts;" *Love and War*, a "musical after-piece;" *Turk and No Turk*, a "musical comedy." To satisfy the growing taste for this fare, the major theaters frequently employed such leading musicians as Thomas Arne, Samuel Arnold, Charles Dibdin, William Shield, Thomas Linley, and Stephen Storace to serve as composers for the theater. Typical of their works regularly advertised in *The Times* were: *The Tempest, Castle of Andalusia, Liberty Hall, Roman Father, The Gentle Shepherd, The Haunted Tower.* Excellent musicians with superior training and extensive experience in instrumental as well as choral music, in performance as well as composition, these men represented the best of the English composers of their generation. That their work had little lasting value is generally conceded, but evidence found in the contemporary *Times* suggests that it was good enough to generate and sustain an extraordinary amount of musical energy and to attract lively and responsive audiences.

The proliferation of this great body of stage m usic, then, w as the result of several factors, one of w hich, as has been pointed out, w as the influence of the peculiar nature of the London theater in shaping public taste. A second factor w as the im pact of the jour- nalistic account of theatrical activities and the burgeoning role of the reporter-review er— the "critic." From the earliest issues of *The Daily Universal Register,* it was clear that, as "friends to the drama" and to music, this paper would often "pronounce opinions on dramatic pieces and performing." Moreover, the policy in "ex- ecuting judgments" was, as defined in the September 19, 1785 issue, "to shew (sic) a liberal disquisition of the merits" and with impartial justice "to point out their beauties as well as their blem- ishes." The intentions of the paper, then, were beyond reproach. As good as these stated intentions were, however, when judged by standards for music criticism which have been refined by genera- tions of journalists over a period of two hundred years, the writers of the reviews did little more than provide an account of the char- acter of the musical performances and a subjective response to their quality.[2]

Though it was only after the appearance of an "outsider," Leigh Hunt (1784-1859), and members of his circle that the musical theater scene was viewed with appreciable objectivity balanced by knowledge of, experience in, and sensitivity to music, there were occasional pieces in *The Times* which did indeed demonstrate well-developed musical taste and sound critical judgment on the part of reporters. During the first two months of *The Daily Universal Register,* several letters which were signed with the pseudonym "Harmonicus" appeared.[3] In the first letter, January 20, 1785, he observes:

> Musical taste and judgment are not only displayed by suiting sound to sentiment, but to the proper accompanying of vocal music; if this be not conducted with the strictest attention, to heighten the intended expression of the song, it destroys it altogether; which frequently happens from the throwing in of full chords, when a single note only should be struck; or, perhaps, when the accompainiment should have ceased altogether.

and this:

> Most performers think they do all that is incumbent on them, if they play in tune and in time, and vanity frequently leads them to make their voice or instrument to be heard above the rest, without attending to the composer's design.

and then:

> Judgment in music is shewn, by adapting

sound to sentiments, and preserving simplicity. Taste in a performer consists in a knowledge of the composer's design, and expressing it in any spirited, (or) pathetic manner, without aiming at shewing the dexterity of his own execution.

and more:

From the whole it may be inferred, that musical genius consists in the invention of melody fitted to produce a desired effect on the mind. Musical taste consists in conducting the melody with spirit and elegance, in such a manner as to produce this single effect in its full force.

On February 4, 1785, a choleric-tempered "Harmonicus" attacks the sadly flawed presentations of the burlettas:

How foreign to ideas of this sort (the qualities of performance commended above) are the starings, skippings, and frequently inharmonious bawling which distinguish burletta representation? It is a just observation that the chief design of these operas, being to gratify the senses and to keep up an indolent attention, painted dragons spitting wild fire might be happily introduced, or fire works played off, and every five minutes little squids or crackers thrown into the boxes, to keep up the attention, when heavy recitatives should go on.

In their daily accounts of stage music, *The Times* reporters most often concerned themselves with the fable (that is, the story), the drama, and the music; the librettist, the composer, the performers and instrumentalists; and the audience. Their columns provide illuminating insights into the public taste of the period. In general, typical judgment passed by a critic rests upon the degree in which the fable is "simple," the cast of characters "strong," and the songs "poetic." Above all, the effect must be "pleasing." An opera characterized by "shrewd observation, wit and pleasantry" is to be commended, and the dialogue abounding with "noble and liberal sentiments" is sure to please. The work should "do honour to genius as well as judgment," and contain nothing which might be construed as "indelicate." Further, such writing should be of "national service by rectifying the minds and improving the people." Newspaper reactions to two comic operas are representative of characteristic responses to this kind of musical presentation. Flaws in the execution of the "fable" of *Strangers at Home* (a pasticcio with some airs by Thomas Linley, libretto by James Cobb) displeased *The Times* critic on December 9, 1785:

> As to the conduct of the Fable, we think it excellent
> in conception, though it sometimes fails in action, ow-
> ing to a redundancy of intrigue, not always novel, and

carried on like the pantomime comedies of the last century by the assistance of disguises, concealments, listenings, and side speeches.

The reviewer thought that the author had broken some of the rules of drama, and for that reason felt that he "was prudent in converting his piece into an Opera, which does not require that strict adherence to nature, and easy rise of incident, indispensably necessary to a comedy." The work of librettist George Colman received particular praise in the July 11, 1785 review of Samuel Arnold's *Turk and No Turk:*

> ... as a work of genius (it) does him infinite credit. The wit bears the sterling stamp of originality, and though not always strictly chaste in its subjects, yet the flashes are so bright, it would be a pity to endanger their lustre by lessening their heat.... The author's intention was clearly to please, and he has succeeded.

It was to the performance of the music that the journalist and the audience reacted most strongly. The presence of "science and taste," "command and execution" in a presentation was noted. "the richness of her melody," "the extent and variety of her cadences" or a voice "full, clear, and capable of great modulation" drew applause. Music should be sung with "great feeling and propriety," and it must "touch the heart." A tenor's performance in

Robin Hood (William Shield, Leonard MacNally) seemed to fulfill all of these expectations, for *The Daily Universal Register's* critic wrote, October 19, 1787, that "his voice is a fine tenor, is perfectly clear and melodious, his manner expressive, and his divisions and cantabiles display a thorough scientific knowledge."

Critics could, however, be very severe. *The Waterman* (music and libretto by Charles Dibdin), performed September 15, 1788, was bluntly described "most miserably performed." Upon seeing one performance of the *Castle of Andalusia* (Samuel Arnold, John O'Keefe), the reviewer, September 24,1789, said "We never witnessed a more imperfect performance — the studied forgetfullness …pervaded the piece." On another occasion, Mr. Williams , having sung the role of Rimenes in *Artaxerxes* (Arne), was advised, April 23, 1788, to omit a particular song "if he cannot make himself more acquainted with the time and the tune." The audience, too, was sensitive to a poor performance, sometimes expressing its sentiments in the form of hissing and shouting, a kind of conduct reporters generally attributed to the galleries.

The reviewers were not entirely without sympathy for performers who were harried by nerves. On one occasion, February 26,1785, a critic regretted that the singer "was so strongly affected with his situation which occasioned a tremor that prevented him from showing his abilities to their extent." Michael Kelly in *Richard Le Coeur de Lion* was described, November 1787, as "every inch a king, after having subdued the terrors of a first performance." And when Mr. Bowden of Manchester sang his first performance in *Robin Hood* (William Shield, Leonard MacNally), the reviewer, October 19,1787, asked that "allowances be made for the terror of a first appearance."

The contribution of the orchestra, less frequently noted than that of the vocal performers, was usually considered in connection with the overture. The reporter might react in general terms to its "varied excellence," describe it as a "masterpiece of composition," or commend its display of "taste and a soundness of judgment." In a letter to the editor, December 23, 1786, "Thespis" asserts that "the music should be of a stile to give an idea of the performance that is to follow, and between every act, it should keep the mind attuned to the succeeding act." Usually in discussions of the overture, some attention is directed to individual performers. For example, in the review of *Marion* (William Shield, Mrs. Brooke), the critic, May 23, 1788, observes that the "Overture gave full scope to the skill and execution of Mr. William Parke's oboe." A November 16, 1785 notice of *Choleric Fathers* contained this encomium for both the overture and its performers:

> The Overture from its varied excellence, is
> a master-piece of composition, and the obligato parts
> are executed with... strength and taste...

Bumgartner's violin, Parke's hautboy, and Serjeant's trumpet would grace the finest band on earth.

Though often singled out for praise, the orchestra and its members were not immune to rebuke. Following a performance of *Love in a Village* (a pasticcio, Bickerstaff librettist), the instrumentalists were informed (February 23, 1788): "the Orchestra in the commencement of the second Act were very much at fault. We forbear particularizing the offence, in perceiving more attention in the future." After attending a production of *Gil Blas* (William Reeve and Bates), a greenroom observer wrote on July 21, 1788: " . . . we recommend to the orchestra more *piano* as his (master Braham's) voice is frequently lost in the music." The critic praised the band for their performance in *The Tempest* (composer unknown, John Kemble librettist) on the night of October 14, 1789, noting that the instrumentalists "were perfectly correct, and the choruses in every respect 'sublime and beautiful'." But there was one flaw: "the HORRID instrumental CRASH that accompanied the sinking of the Banquet was only instrumental to raising a laugh in the Orchestra as well as the House—and totally destroyed the effect it was meant to have produced."

Two reviews, one unfavorable and the other largely favorable, will provide illustrations of typical stage music criticism written for *The Daily Universal Register/London Times*. Each account notices most of the elements to which contemporary audiences and critics usually reacted. To the reviewer of *The Siege of Curzola* (composer unknown, John O'Keefe librettist) on August 14, 1786, the drama was virtually without merit — structureless, ill-proportioned, and filled with vulgarities and plagiarisms. Plainly, O'Keefe, skilled in farce, had overreached himself in attempting a form of drama from which moral instruction as well as humor was expected and for which his talents were unsuited. Spirited, able, and diligent as the individual performers were, they could not make a poor opera go. Nevertheless, the reporter rounded his account with quite specific recommendations for improving the piece and its performance. Apparently, a discriminating audience concurred with the critic's judgment of the quality of the production, for the play, first presented on August 12, 1786, was not repeated until July 2, 1787, and only two other performances, on July 4 and July 9, followed. In marked contrast, the critic reviewing *The Haunted Tower,* a pasticcio with original music by Stephen Storace, found almost every aspect of the production pleasing and judged the opening night (November 24, 1789) to be highly successful. The reporter praised Mr. Cobb, librettist, for "the plot, interest, and incidents," and for the "neatness of the dialogue, both in its comic and serious passages." Of the music and the performance of various singers, the writer observed:

> The new and old music does great credit to the composition and selection of Storace — the overture has

many passages which even GLUCK might not be ashamed to own; that the airs were held in the estimation they deserved, the frequent encores sufficiently testified.

He spoke of the "exquisite powers" of Anna Storace and noted particular airs of Mrs. Crouch and Mr. Kelly which "abounded with the sublime and beautiful." By December 31st, the entertainment had been repeated eighteen times, an indication of approval by audience and critics alike.

From the records of *The Daily Universal Register/London Times*, it is plain that London audiences enjoyed a great variety and a great quantity of stage music in the 1780's. Ninety different works were announced in *The Times* from its first edition January 1, 1785 through December 31, 1789.[4] The total number of presentations, including repetitions, as noted in *The Times* came to roughly 1355, a figure which attests to the continuous popularity of this form of entertainment. The columns of the daily newspaper are revealing chronicles of these musical events. A relatively new addition to the newspaper organization, the reporter-reviewers, writing anonymously, seem to have been diligent in their pursuits. Lacking the distinction of the literary style of later music critics, they sought to communicate straightforward appraisals of what they saw and heard in the musical theatre. The daily columns of *The*

Times provide this multifaceted view of the musical climate in which this popular entertainment prospered.

FOOTNOTES

[1]There were two other theatres which occupied a position some-where between that of the major theatres and that of the lesser theatres. One was the King's Theatre, which was used for the Italian Opera. The other, the Haymarket, had a unique license or patent which limited its season to that time when Drury Lane and Covent Garden were closed (usually during the summer), though special dispensation could be granted by the Lord Chamberlain for out-of-the-ordinary presentations. See Charles Beecher Hogan, *The London Stage 1776-1800, An Introduction* (Carbondale and Edwardsville: Southern Illinois University Press, 1968), pp. cxxviii-cxxxiii.

[2]Not until 1805 can the identity of *The Times* theatre critics be established with certainty. According to *The History of the Times,* John Walter, founder, was followed by John Walter II who "consistently man-aged (from 1803-1808) the theatrical criticism. . . in consonance with the... principles of Leigh Hunt . . . " (I, 90). Over the years the combina-tion of such figures as Barron Field, a member of the Hunt circle, Leigh Hunt, George Croly, William Hazlitt left a remarkable impact upon criti-cism. But it was only in 1846 that *The Times*, the first English newspaper to do so, appointed a professionally trained music critic: James W. Davison. (II, 443). See *The History of the Times.* 4 vols. (London: The Office of *The Times*, 1935-1952), Vols. I and 11. See also Theodore Finney, *"Mak-ing of an Opera Critic: Leigh Hunt,"* Musical Quarterly, LV (October, 1969) 439-463; *Edmund Blunden, Leigh Hunt and His Circle* (New York and London: Harper and Brothers, 1930).

[3]The use of pseudonyms such as Thespis, Criticus, Theatricus, Roscius, Harmonicus in the early newspaper's columns was frequent, stem-ming perhaps from the chance that suits for libel or slander might arise from unpopular opinions. Usually, however, music reports were then as today, simply incorporated in columns called "London News," "Theatri-cal Intelligence," "Musical Intelligence" or in undesignated columns of greenroom gossip.

[4]Since twenty-seven issues of *The Daily Universal Register* in

the first six months of 1785 were missing from the micro-film, it is probable that numbers of performances were in fact much greater than this study reveals. See The Record of *The Times* Newspaper London. (Recordak Division of Kodak Limited, London, England).

Smaller Ensemble
as Well as Larger Orchestral Accomplishments

In this study of *The Times*, it has been shown how greatly enhanced the late 18th century music enthusiasts were becoming with the variety and excellence being offered to the ever-growing audiences. Stage music was at this time of great importance in the music scene. The English operas, variously announced in *The Times* as comic operas, musical comedies, pastoral operas, burlettas, pasticcios and adaptations, were produced in endless succession at Covent Garden, Drury Lane, and the Haymarket; in the first six months of 1785, more than one hundred twenty-five performances of these plays were presented at these three theatres. That Italian Opera in London was a flourishing enterprise is reflected in *The Times* record of more than two hundred twenty-five presentations from 1785-1789. Secure in drawing major virtuosi from the continent to sing the leading roles in operas by such composers as Paesiello, Cimarosa, and Tarchi, the King's Theatre easily garnered its share of the London audience; "bumper houses" were assured. Large-scale vocal and choral works presented almost weekly attracted widespread interest, and the oratorio, long revered in the great city, was probably, of all musical activities, the most eagerly awaited. The Lenten season brought forth the traditional oratorio performances at Covent Garden, Drury Lane, and Tottenham Street Rooms. Throngs of people attended.

Increasing reports and appraisals on the part of the journalists coincided with these activities, and, while reporters of musical events, writing for the most part anonymously, were a relatively new addition to newspaper staffs, writers for *The Times*, in their frank reactions to what they saw and heard, provide illuminating insights into the musical taste and practices of the period. First called *The Daily Universal Register*, the newly established *Times* (1785), adventurous, energetic, and forthright in character, is a fresh, hitherto virtually unexplored avenue for a study of this period in London's music history. The complex portrait of the music scene and of the people responsible for it is to be found in reports of events taking place, in "Letters" and essays, in announcements, in green-room gossip. Published daily, innumerable programs of the major and minor theatres, of membership societies, of vocalists and instrumentalists appearing in concerts both public and private, attest to the abundance and variety of musical activity. Eager to support Londoners' interest in music, John Walter, founder of *The Times*, promised: "… the Italian Opera, oratorio, every concert and Musical Meeting of reputation shall be attended to." He kept his promise. Through the paper's daily columns, the essential character of the London music scene, 1785-1789, becomes clearly apparent.

Vying in popularity with the Italian Opera, the English operas, the Lenten oratorios, and the great festivals in London and the provinces, the varied forms of concert music attracted a large share of attention from the London music audience. While eminent instrumentalists made up the "band," which contributed the essential accompaniments to the operatic and oratorio programs, they further enhanced these performances by playing "overtures," or concertos, or instrumental solos between the acts or between the choral numbers. But the concert room, private or public, without the distractions of elaborate theatrical trappings gave the instrumentalists --- and vocalists --- another avenue for artistic achievement and provided the London musical scene with another significant dimension.

Subscription concerts, enjoying a tradition which dated from the early part of the century, flourished during the second half of the 1780's. The most famous were the Professional Concerts at Hanover Square, Salomon's Concerts, Mara's Concerts, the Pantheon Concerts, the Freemason Hall Subscriptions, and a short-lived series which combined poetry reading and music. Benefit concerts abounded in the late winter and spring, and soloists obligingly lent their talents for the artistic and financial rewards of a friend's "night." Charity benefits, such as the annual one for the General Lying-In Hospital, profited from royal patronage. Music societies whose membership included amateur performers from the nobility and gentry were made more attractive by the inclusion of professional musicians in their ranks. Most prestigious of these musical organizations were the Academy of Antient Music, the

Concert of Ancient Music. and the more convivial but none-the-less serious Anacreontic Society. While policies relating to the selections of music for their programs differed, the members of these groups were dedicated to the music of the most esteemed composers, performed by highly reputed musicians. Numerous private concerts were provided by the wealthy. Their morning concerts, Sunday evening concerts, and Ladies' Concerts were an important part of the musical scene. Able musicians, particularly those who were visitors from the continent, were repeatedly invited to perform at Marlborough, Buckingham, Carlton House, or Hinchinbroke as soloists or in ensembles, groups which were sometimes augmented by competent musicians from the household. During the summer months, among the most popular attractions for Londoners who thronged to the famous pleasure gardens --- Vauxhall and Ranelagh --- were the public concerts. As Editor John Walter promised, in an early statement of the newspaper's policy, *The London Times* continuously publicized these events and permanently recorded the critics' reaction to them.

The number and quality of the musicians who performed with the various concerts are extensively attested to by daily reports, reviews, and notices appearing in *The Times*. Further, the newspaper's accounts make abundantly clear London's increasing interest in the "concert." There are frequent observations to the effect that "music is the rage everywhere," a rage "which pervades all ranks and degrees," ranging from "the Sunday concerts which are becoming quite the *ton* with the great ones," to the "very elegant concert given a few evenings ago at the butcher's near Leadenhall-market." Indeed, the concert fever of the spring of 1786 had reached such a pitch that one commentator, responding to the projected Vauxhall and Ranelagh programs, declared the music audience to be "sated with concerts --- spiritual and temporal --- and fatigued with orchestras without end."

Assessment of group performers and performances is more difficult. Contrary, however, to the late Marion Scott's conclusion that "music was fashionable because the Royal Family were keen amateurs," that the music world was made up of "scores of clever musicians," that quantity was mistaken for quality,[1] a study of *The London Times* clearly reveals a society, however stratified, genuinely fond of music in its many forms, and a wealth of excellent musicians dedicated to their artistic pursuits. The latter quarter of the eighteenth century in England was distinguished by such musical figures as J. C. Bach and K. F. Abel, by Muzio Clementi, the Cramers --- father and son; by Pachierotti, Madame Mara, and Nancy Storace, who sang the role of Susanna in the first performance of *Le Nozzi di Figaro* in Vienna; by Dr. Arne, Dr. Arnold, and William Shield, violinist, composer and friend of Haydn--and by the impresario, Johann Peter Salomon. Moreover, this was the world into which, following Salomon's successful coup in arranging for his visit, the great Haydn moved in January 1791 — "the large, excellently trained orchestras" at his disposal, Geiringer surmises, having been a deciding factor in Haydn's decision to come to England.[2] These were the instrumentalists who provided the means by which an era of great activity in orchestral performance in England was to be opened.

As has been noted, among the most distinguished and influential forms of concert performances in the period 1785-1789 were the subscription concert series. The largest and the most prestigious of these musical functions took place at the Hanover Square Rooms. These programs grew out of the Abel and Bach weekly concerts which began in 1764. Coming from Germany in 1759 and 1762, respectively, these two musicians joined the ranks of foreigners who for some time had been bringing music styles and practices across the channel, and their contributions were significant additions to the music scene. Mrs. Teresa Cornelys induced the two friends to conduct a subscription series at her elegant Assembly-Rooms, the first taking place on January 23, 1765. Enormously successful, these concerts continued until the end of 1767 when a rival establishment, Almack's, won Abel's and Bach's services.[3]

In 1774, Abel and Bach entered into a partnership with John Gallini, an Italian dancing-master and later colorful manager of the King's Theatre, and the three of them bought a house and a site of land on the east side of Hanover Square.[4] On February 1, 1775, Bach and Abel played a joint concert which opened the new Hanover Square Rooms, destined to become famous as a setting for music concerts for almost a century. The subscription series continued until Bach's death in 1782. Abel returned to Germany for a period of time, and in his absence Lord Abingdon, the "Maecenas of Music" as he came to be called by *The Times*, endeavored to keep the concerts alive, but lack of success led him to withdraw his patronage. In 1783, a few of the instrumentalists, led by Wilhelm Cramer, joined together to give "professional" concerts in these rooms. It is with this series that the curtain opens on this segment of the London musical scene of 1785-1789 as it is pictured in *The Times*.

In his <u>Memoirs,</u> W. T. Parke notes that on February 2, 1785, the Hanover Square Concerts for the first time presented its program under the name Professional Concerts.[5] Taking place on Monday nights in a series of twelve programs, the Professional Concerts were given from late January or early February through April. The first notice by the fledgling newspaper, *The Daily Universal Register* (which became in 1788 *The London Times*), appeared on February 23, 1785, in the announcement for the third concert. Following customs of the day, the program was divided into two "acts;" vocal pieces were alternated with the instrumental music. Typically, neither titles of the songs nor names of their composers were supplied. The program was:

Act I. New Sinfonie, Mr. Abel

    Song, Signor Tenducci

    Solo Violin, Signor Lolli

    Song, Signora Ferrarese

    Concerto for two French Horns, Messrs. Bachs

    Song, Signora Ferrarese

    Concerto Hautboy, Mr. Fischer

Act II. Sinfonie, Haydn

    Song, Signora Ferrarese

    Concerto Hautboy, Mr. Fischer

    Song, Signor Tenducci

    Duetto for two French Horns, Messrs. Bachs[6]

    Overture in Ariadne, Handel

N.B. The Concert will begin precisely at 8 o'clock

    Mr. Abel is engaged   as principal composer.

Two aspects of this program have particular significance: first, the predominance of instrumental music and second, the choice of composers represented in the music selected --- Abel, a great favorite of the period as a performer of the viola da gamba; Bach, foremost composer, harpsichordist, and teacher; Haydn, whose music had been known in England since the 1770's;[7] and Handel, whose name had long been revered. Music by such composers as these appears repeatedly on concert programs, as a close study of *The Times*, 1785-1789, reveals. Further, from this study, it is apparent that interest in contemporary music predominated and that much of the "new music" has survived for two centuries --- a fact reflecting rather remarkable critical judgment on the part of the program planners.

In the ten Professional Concerts programs published by *The Times,* Haydn's works, varying from an "overture" or "symphony" to the "New Quartetto, M. S., for Two Violins, Tenor and Violoncello," appeared eight times[9] --- twice on the February 2, 1789 concert. Bach was represented in programs which included his *"Overture, Double Orchestra,"* a *"Quintetto for Violin, Piano Forte, Tenor and Violoncello,"* and a *"Divertemente for two Violins, two Haut boys, two Tenors, and two French Horns."* Abel's compositions, usually a "symphony," one a "concertante," were played on five programs. Pleyel's name, first seen on a 1787 program, appears twice on the February 11, 1788 concert, and again a year later. Among the instrumental compositions, Handel's name is found three times only. Mozart's music was represented by a "New Overture" on February 11, 1788, and an "Overture" on February 2, 1789. Other instrumental compositions were chosen from the works of Clementi, Piehl, Pfeiffer, and Rosetti.

Instrumentalists performing with the Professional Concerts

were announced in the January 24, 1787 issue of *The Times*. The list is interesting not only for the names of the performers "for the ensuing year," but also for the indication of the divisions within the orchestra:

> Composer, Mr. Abel. Leader of the Band, Mr. Cramer
>
> Singers: Signor Rubinelli, Mrs. Billington,
>   Miss Cecelia Davies
>
> First Violins: Messrs. Salpietro, Soderini, Shield, Cordell,
>   and Agus
>
> Second Violins: Messrs: Borghi, Gehot, Parkinson,
>   Vidini, Howard and Lanzoni
>
> Tenors: Blake, Napier, Hackwood, and Rawlings
>
> Violoncellos: Cervetto, Sharp and King, Scola, and Smith
>
> Double Basses: Gariboldi, Sharp, and King
>
> Harpsichord: Mr. Dance
>
> Hautboys: Messrs. Park and Huttley
>
> Flutes: Messrs. Florio and Decamp
>
> Horns: Pieltain and OKelly
>
> Bassoons: Baumgarten and J. Parkinson[10]

The omission of Johann Peter Salomon's name is notable --- an absence which further corroborates the fact that he had already separated himself from the Professional Concerts. Salomon, of course, began his own series on March 2, 1786. It is particularly surprising that *The Times*, consistently eager to cover every facet of instrumental music (vocal as well), published no advertisement or review of his subscription concerts. It is especially strange since Salomon's performances for the benefits of his colleagues and for his own benefits and his appearances on various programs both in and outside of London were given excellent notices by *The Times* reporters.

While *The Times* ignored the Salomon series, the paper provided thorough coverage for the concerts in Mme. Mara's subscription series. Indeed, the paper seldom lost the opportunity to keep the public informed of the activities of this extraordinary woman whose musical abilities and personal charm attracted attention at home and abroad. Gossip columns, announcements of the programs, and critical reports kept her name before the public. In 1787, she launched her own subscription concerts at the Pantheon. The particular success of the 1788 series was assured by the engagement of such well-known singers and instrumental soloists as: Michael Kelly and Mrs. Pieltain; Graff, Ashley, Mons. Mara, Hindmarsh, Fischer, Ponto, and Raimondi (who was also to be the conductor).

Though she was the leading soprano of the period, Mara's concerts emphasized instrumental rather than vocal music. Each program began with an "overture" and almost unfailingly ended with a "full piece;" sometimes, the second act also began with a "symphony." With particular interest in concertos, she placed no fewer than twenty-eight concertos on the ten 1788 programs published by *The Times:* ten for the hautboy were played by Fischer; seven for French horn were performed by Ponto; six for violin were presented by Raimondi; for four flute concertos Graff was the soloist, and for one tenor concerto, Mons. Mara was the principal instrumentalist. In addition to the concertos, there were eleven "overtures," seven of which were by Haydn. Furthermore, there were ten "ensemble" pieces: two quintets, one trio, and six quartettos, one of these by Haydn for "two violins, tenor, and violoncello."

A second major series of musical programs given at the Pantheon bore the name of the hall itself. Opened in 1772, this lavishly designed place of public amusement provided Londoners with a sumptuous setting for masqued balls, suppers with wine, and concerts during the cold months of the year as did Vauxhall and Ranelagh in the summer time. The concerts were given in the magnificent Rotunda.[11]

On February 13, 1786, *The Times* printed its first announcement for the Pantheon series: "The nobility and gentry are respectfully acquainted that there will be a CONCERT at this place, on THURSDAY next, the 16th Instant, and be continued on every succeeding Thursday." Two principal singers were named: Mrs.

Barthelemon and Mrs. Arrowsmith. The orchestra was to be under the direction of Mr. Barthelemon. No further mention is made of the 1786 season's subscription, but on November 27 of the same year, a similar announcement was made for the opening "tomorrow night." The programs were to be "continued every succeeding Tuesday during the Season." To the two previously announced singers were added "Messrs. Sale, Billington, Chapman and Salmon." The "admittance" was announced to be "Three Shillings and Sixpence each Person; or Tickets at the Office." The first of the 1786-1787 concerts was presented on November 28, and the program for each of the series running weekly through February 27 was regularly announced on the first page of *The Times*.

The structure of the eleven programs studied followed in general the prevailing pattern of a first and second act, the first number of each act being an "overture," and the conclusion of the second act being a "full piece." A particular distinction in the Pantheon Concerts is found in the final piece of the first act and in the number prior to the concluding "full piece" in the second act; these numbers were invariably a "glee" and a "catch," most frequently drawn from Purcell or Arne. Inclusion of these pieces, while balancing almost evenly the vocal and instrumental works, lengthened the programs to as many as fifteen numbers! Mara's programs ran to nine or ten; the Professional Concerts, usually eleven. Haydn and Abel were each played six times, Corelli four, and Stamitz three. Thirteen other composers were represented: Handel, Bach, Graff, Geminiani, Martini, Barthelemon, Vanhall, Vanmaldere --- all twice each; Avison, Sarmata, Filtz, Ricci, and Torschi, once each. While concertos were not so frequent as in the other subscription concerts, there were on these eleven programs ten for violin, and six concertos or "duettos" for French horn played by the Leander brothers. The following program which opened the 1786-1787 season is typical of those presented in the Pantheon series:

Act I.

Overture, Vanmaldere

Song, Mr. Arrowsmith

Concerto Grosso, Avison

Song, Mrs. Barthelemon

Concerto, French Horns, the Leanders

Glee, "Sweet Muse," Dr. Arne

(By desire) the Catch of Purcell's,

"The bonny Christ Church Bells"

Act II.

A New Overture

Song, Mr. Sale

(By desire) the New Concerto as performed last

Tuesday by Mr. Barthelemon

Song, Mr. Arrowsmith

Song, Mrs. Barthelemon

Glee, "Here in the Cool Grot," by the late Lord

Mornington

Favourite Catch, "Mr. Speaker, tho 'tis late"

Full Piece, Bach[12]

The Freemasons' Hall was the locale for still another distinctive subscription series. Opened in May 1776, this building, designed for the purposes of the Freemasons' organization, was the scene of many concerts and benefits. The Academy of Antient Music met here from 1784 until 1792. According to Robert Elkin, the hall played "a modest but not negligible part in London's music."[13]

The unusual Freemasons' series which combined literary readings and music was initiated in August 1786 through two apparently exploratory entertainments under the management of Mr. Lacy. The programs on August 11 and August 30 were warmly received by *The Times* critics. A September 27th announcement in the paper indicated ambitious programs to come. Beginning November 18, there were to be "six nights" (in addition, two extra programs under a different management were announced February 25 and March 3); the subscriptions were to be limited to three hundred members and the admission was to be one guinea each subscriber. The readings were to be selected from Ossian, Milton, Dryden, Pope, Swift, Thomson, Fielding, Richardson, Young, Sterne, Grey, Colman, Garrick, Sheridan, Jerningham, Walcot, Pratt, Miss Burney, Charlotte Smith, Miss Seward, and "occasional new writings." Both instrumental and operatic music were to be chosen from composers whose works, judging from the frequency of references to them in *The Times*, seemed to be particularly attractive to the audiences of this period: Morley, Locke, Purcell, Handel, Corelli, Geminiani, Arne, Boyce, Howard, Morgan, Arnold, Cook, Bach, Abel, Haydn, Sacchini, Bertini, Jackson, Linley, Carter, Barthelemon, Hook, Webb, Shield, Giordani, Sarti, Anfossi, and Mortellari.

The nine programs printed in *The Times* indicate that the musical portions of these composite concerts were in many ways similar to the programs of the other subscriptions. "Overtures" were chosen from Arne, Gluck, and Haydn. In four out of the nine presentations, the concluding number was a "Grand Overture" by Haydn --- indeed on December 16, 1786, the finale to the first act as well as to the second was also a Haydn "Grand Overture." Handel was frequently performed: one concluding "Full Piece," an "Hautboy Concerto," a "Second Hautboy Concerto," a "Grand Concerto," and the "Fifth Grand Concerto." Corelli's "Eighth Concerto," Avison's "Concerto," Hoffman's "Concertante for Violin, Tenor, and Violoncello," Giornovichi's "Concerto, Violin," and Pleyel's "Quartetto," as well as "new music by Mr. Billington" were all presented. On several occasions, Mr. Billington played the pianoforte to accompany Miss Leary and Signor Sestini. On other programs, accompaniments by Mr. Huttley on the hautboy, Mr. Potter on the flute, and Mr. Mahon on the clarinet were praised by the critic as "distinguished."

Significant concert series were also provided through three active musical societies --- the Academy of Antient Music, Concerts of Ancient Music, and the Anacreontic Society. The oldest of these membership organizations was the Academy, established in 1726. Motivated by a strong interest in vocal and instrumental music, its membership was drawn from distinguished professionals and amateurs. In 1787, *The Times* spoke of the "list of candidates upon the Society's books" as containing "upwards of seventy names of the most respectable gentlemen in London and Westminster." Its earliest director was Dr. Pepusch. Over the years its members met at the Crown and Anchor Tavern until 1784 when it moved to the spacious quarters of the Freemasons' Hall. Traditionally, the society met fortnightly. Various members of the society planned the concerts, a custom also followed by the two other membership organizations. Upon one occasion, the music was selected by a Mr. Smith, upon another by Albert Jones, Esq., and on still another by James Madden.

During the period 1785-1789, the Academy's interest seems to have been predominantly in vocal music. In their programs as in others where this was major fare, much of the music was drawn from Handel. While such earlier composers as Pergolesi and Byrd were often performed, contemporary or near-contemporary composers were also heard --- Dr. Arne was a great favorite. Programs were printed in *The Times* as parts of reviews, located usually on page two or three.[14] Extracted from a report written December 28, 1787, the following concert, planned by Peter Stapel, Esq., serves as an example of the musical taste and interests of this organization.

> *Act I.*
>
>> Overture to Atalanta
>> Italian Canzonet --- Dr. Cooke
>> Italian Air from Sacchini
>> Concerto --- Martini, Op. 8
>> Old Madrigal by Weelks
>> Te Deum – Graun
>
> *Act II.*
>
>> First Concerto -- Geminiani
>> Madrigal --- Hutchinson
>> Quartetto --- Sacchini
>> Aria from Jeptha
>> Eighth Concerto --- Corelli
>> Aria from Jeptha
>> Chorus from Jeptha

The 1787-1788 series (the specific dates were published in *The Times*, October 30, 1787) ran for twelve meetings scheduled from November 29 through May 1. Elkins records that the subscription fee was "Five Guineas admitting one Gentleman and Two Ladies, each night of the concert"[15] According to the newspaper reporters' estimates, the number of members and guests attending the concerts ranged from three hundred to as many as seven hundred.

In reviews, usually quite generous in length, *The Times* critics' reactions were generally mild and quite respectful; a program was "noble, musical and beautiful," or a performance was "truly superlative." The audience for the December 18, 1789 opening of the winter season was declared to be "brilliant and fashionable" --- an easy cliché frequently resorted to by columnists. The selection of pieces for this particular evening was made by the Duke of Leeds. Dr. Arnold, the Director from 1789-1792, was at the organ, and Salomon was the leader of the band, both "most excellent in their departments."[16] The critic called attention to the fact that "no expense seems to have been spared to render the concert equal to any in London," and added that the orchestra was "very full." According to Sandys and Forster, the actual size of the 1789 Academy of Antient Music band and the distributions of the parts were "one organ, fourteen violins, Barthelemon being the first, four violas, four violoncellos, three hautboys, two trumpets, two horns, three bassoons, two double bassoons, and one drum."[17]

A second prestigious society, the Concert of Ancient Music, was organized in 1776. This socially elite group was directed by a number of noblemen, among whom were the Earl of Sandwich, the Earl of Exeter, the Earl of Urbridge, and Sir William Watkins Wynn, Baronet. The Concert's prestige was increased in 1785 when the king and the royal family gave their support to the programs by their attendance --- whence the additional title, King's Concerts. The meetings were held at the Tottenham Street Rooms, which, built in 1772 by Francis Pasquali, were variously known as Pasquali's Rooms, the New Rooms, the Ancient Concert Rooms, and Tottenham Street Rooms.[18] Here, interested audiences gathered to listen to music by "venerable composers" such as Purcell, Corelli, Gluck, Pergolesi, and certainly Handel. Society policy required that the music, selected by one of the members, should have been composed at least twenty years previous. Performing the music, Burney reminisced, was a "select and powerful band."[19] Parke mentions Bates "at the organ," with Cramer leading the band.[20]

In comparison with the attention given by the paper to the Academy of Antient Music concerts, the interest shown by *The Times* in the Ancient Concerts programs was slight. Notices were infrequent and brief; critical reactions were often indifferent and occasionally caustic.[21] The records frequently indicate a disapproval of the society's total concentration upon "old music." In the March

15, 1786 edition, one columnist wrote: "The Directors of Ancient Music may be compared to the character in the Comedy who declares he paid three hundred pounds a year to keep his <u>ruins</u> in repair --- To preserve the national music is undoubtedly a worthy object, but this should not go only to the collecting, to improve it should be the great end." "There is nothing in the Concert of Antient (sic) Music which surprises us, but Lord Sandwich's attachment to it. Is it since he is grown old himself, that he is fond of antient <u>pieces</u>?" observed another reporter in the February 22, 1787 issue. Written for the November 17, 1787 paper, the review of a Rehearsal ("Rehearsals" for which there was an admission charge seemed to have some of the significance of today's "preview") showed a more generous than usual reaction to one of the programs:

> The Rehearsal for the first night (Thursday se 'night) was performed on Thursday evening, before a very numerous body of the subscribers; and, from the bill of fare, a rich treat may be expected at the ensuing meeting.

> Mr. Barthelemon leads; we were happy to find that his powers are not impaired.

> The concert began with the overture of Esther, the various movements of which were given in a very masterly stile.

> "Come all noble souls," --- Rogers, was most correctly and elegantly sung by Wilson, Hebler, and

Sale. Miss T. Abrams, in the absence of her elder sister, sang, "What though I trace each herb and flower," in such a sweet and pleasing taste, that we for the moment forgot the absence of her sister. Doctor Cooke's glee of the epitaph upon a Dormouse "in paper case," was next sung; there is such a richness in the adagio, that it never fails to interest the passions. The first act closed with a Latin mass, composed by Pergolesi. in which the chorus was very well sustained.

The second act opened with the 9th grand concerto; after which Doctor Arne's glee, "Come Shepherds, let's follow the Hearse," was performed, in remembrance of the late Mr. Paxton, who was for many years one of the band. "There is a kind of melancholy suavity, a luxury of sorrow, which runs through the whole of this glee, that it never fails to make a deep impression upon the audience."

A Chorus from Athalia, "The mighty Powers," was given with a grandeur of style, which belongs to that wonderful composition. --- Several other pieces were performed, and at half after ten the rehearsal closed, very much to the satisfaction of the subscribers with William Bird's famous canon, <u>Non Nobis Domine.</u>[22]

The Times' enthusiasm for the productions of the third membership organization, the Anacreontic Society, was unequivocal. In the seventh issue of the new *Daily Universal Register* (January 8, 1785), a third of a column was devoted to a report on the "Anacreontic Meeting." The article concluded: "In short, it must be said that for elegance of company, joined to elegance of music and song, the Anacreontic takes the lead of all other musical meetings in Europe." A little excessive, perhaps, but close study of the society's activities as they subsequently are described in *The Times* does suggest a high degree of excellence in the choice of music presented and in the performance by, as Parke who became a member in 1786 said, "the flower of the musical profession."[23] Founded in 1766, this fashionable society limited its membership, but members were privileged to introduce friends. Meetings were held fortnightly in the great ballroom of the Crown and Anchor Tavern (home of the Academy of Antient Music in its earlier days). The assemblages were large, *The Times* reporting upon occasion "upwards of two hundred gentlemen," or "three hundred," or at another meeting "near four hundred strong." Catches, glees, songs, toasts, and the traditional singing of the Anacreontic Hymn after the "grand concert," along with a good supper, undoubtedly added to the attractions of the meetings, but these convivialities seem not to have detracted from serious attention to the music of both the old masters and the new.

Although *The Times* provided no advance announcements of the organization's meetings, reporters gave excellent coverage of the meetings, describing the programs, calling attention to particular instrumentalists, and offering critical reactions to the music and musicians. They frequently mentioned performances by such popular figures as Clementi, the greatly admired harpsichordist and pianofortist; Parke, the hautboyist; Mahon, the clarinetist; and Blake who played the tenor. Occasionally, critics seemed interested in encouraging young and talented performers, noting on one occasion that Cramer, Jr. "distinguished himself in a harpsichord lesson of Mozart's" and observing at another time that the young man "exerted those wonderful abilities, which, guided by prudence, cannot fail to place him in the highest seat of his profession." The Leander brothers were praised for their performance of a concerto for horns, but at the same time were admonished "to attend to their subject with strictness, and not let exertion overpower reason and judgment."

The Anacreontic programs differed somewhat from the concerts of the various subscriptions series and those of the Antient Music and the Ancient Concerts. Programs were shorter, presumably because some of the evening's entertainment was apparently devoted to group singing of popular songs. Emphasis was placed upon instrumental music, with the inclusion of one or possibly two vocal solos by some well known singer such as Michael Kelly, Mr. Dignum, or Mr. Sedgwick. A typical program consisted of two or three "overtures" or symphonies, several concertos, and one or two instrumental ensembles. Compositions by Handel, Geminiani, and Martini were occasionally programmed, but interest in the old masters was far exceeded by that in contemporary composers. Rosetti and Kozeluch were frequently performed; Pleyel quartettos and Clementi's pianoforte sonatas were popular.

The two most significant contemporary composers represented on the Anacreontic programs were Haydn and Mozart. In *The Times* reviews studied, Haydn's name appears most often. Many of the concerts began with one of his "overtures" or closed with one of his "grand symphonies." A reporter wrote on January 4, 1788 --- with the approbation Haydn constantly received --- "The concert commenced with a new overture by Haydn, distinguished by all the brilliancy and masterly effect, characteristic of that composer. Two others by the same author were also performed, equally distinguished by their peculiar excellence. It is unnecessary to remark that these exquisite performances are the same as dedicated to his Royal Highness the Prince of Wales, and Opera 51 of Haydn, and different from anything heretofore published by that author." At a later meeting, a "new overture . . . from the last set of symphonies dedicated to His Royal Highness, the Duke of York" was performed; two of the movements were said to be "remarkably fine."[24] On the same program a second symphony of Haydn's "went off with an extraordinary degree of <u>eclat</u>."

The frequency with which Mozart's music appears on the Anacreontic programs, particularly for the 1787 and 1788 meetings, further attests to the preference of the society's members for contemporary music. The third concert in this season (November 7, 1787) opened and closed with symphonies by Mozart; the first, "a new symphony by Mozart . . . was well received and had great merit"; the second was judged to be "very inferior to the first."[25] At the following December meeting, "an Overture by Mozart was first introduced, the effort of which was sensibly felt ..." Programs in 1788 included a "Symphony, Op. 8," a "Grand Overture," a "manuscript Symphony of Mozart's (which) was not only new, but contained some excellent movements." On November 14, 1788, *The Times* reported a recent program which included "a new trio for the Pianoforte, Violin, and Tenor by Mozart ... admirably performed by Messrs. Clementi, Cramer, and Blake."[26]

In late eighteenth century London, the famous pleasure gardens of Ranelagh and Vauxhall were scenes of additional concerts which, in the summer months, drew great crowds of people from all classes of society. Here, music competed with fireworks, exhibitions, picnics, promenades, regattas, masquerades, and ridottos for the attention of the public. While, on occasion, musicians "strolled" through the park, the more formal programs provided by orchestras of leading instrumentalists and singers were usually held in the elegant Rotundas. Audiences assembled to listen to professional performances of Handel, Geminiani, Bach, Haydn, Paesiello, to concertos and sonatas, to oratorios and symphonies, to excerpts from favorite operas, to catches and glees.

But the study of *The Times* reveals very slim records of music at Ranelagh from 1785-1789. This famous garden,[27] according to Mollie Sands, historian of Ranelagh,[28] reached the peak of its popularity during the mid-seventies and soon thereafter began its decline in "fashion" and "in the quality of its music." *The Times* often referred to the state of the park, "once a place of fashion," now "neglected by the managers." One reporter noted in 1788 that "In respect to amusement there was none." However, according to Miss Sands, the fortunes of the park were entering a period of recovery by 1790. Indeed, during the preceding year the paper reported a renewal of activities and entertainments at the park, as part of the festivities planned throughout the city honoring the king's recovery from illness. On April 13, 1789, *The Times* announced the summer series of Monday-Wednesday-Friday concerts of vocal and instrumental music which were to continue through August. Only the first of these programs was published:

Act I

 Overture Occasional, Handel

 Fourth Concerto, Avison

 Song, Mr. Griffiths

 Overture, Haydn

 Song, Miss Mahon

 Concerto, French horn, Messrs. Leanders

 Coronation Anthem,

 God Save the King with full chorus on the Joyful
  RESTORATION OF HIS MAJESTY'S HEALTH

Act II

 Overture, Acis and Galatea, with the chorus,
  "O the Pleasure of the Plains"

 Concerto, clarinet, Mr. Mahon

 Overture, Bach

 Song, Mr. Griffiths

 Overture, Haydn

 Concerto violin, Mr. Ashley, Junior

 Song, Miss Mahon

  To conclude with

 God Save Great George Our King, with full chorus

For the period 1785-1789, Vauxhall was in fashion, and its music activities were flourishing. In the summers of 1786 and 1787, the programs were regularly published for the concerts which were given Tuesday, Thursday, and Saturday nights from the end of May through August. Hook was the director, organist, and composer. For 1786 the vocalists included Mrs. Martyr, Miss Burnett, Miss Leary, and Mr. and Mrs. Incledon. Among the instrumental soloists were Parke and Pieltain, at least one of whom played a concerto for each program; Parkinson, bassoonist, who played for six programs; the Leander brothers, who played a concerto. On each program Hook played an organ concerto. For the Prince's birthday program Serjeant presented a trumpet concerto.

Hook divided the programs into two acts as was customary and followed the pattern set at the Pantheon by ending the first act with glees and catches. The first act was long, with eleven or twelve numbers exclusive of the glees and catches; the second act included three solos followed by the finale. The finale was usually one of Hook's own compositions, his <u>Triumph of Beauty</u> being the most popular. Occasionally, a "New Finale" was played.

On the fifty-nine programs for the summers of 1786 and 1787 printed in *The Times*, Haydn continued to be the most popular composer, represented on thirty-three out of thirty-five concerts in 1786 and twenty-two out of twenty-four in 1787. At Vauxhall, Handel's instrumental music held its own with Haydn's, with fifty-five appearances on fifty-nine programs. Bach's music was heard on twenty-nine programs; Stamitz', on twenty-four of the fifty-nine. Hook programmed his own compositions (exclusive of his finales) for fourteen occasions, Arne's music for twelve. Richter's "overtures" or "symphonies" were performed eight times, as also were Abel's compositions. Boyce, Vanhal, Ditters were played five and six times, and Guglielmi, Rush, and Lord Kelly several times each summer. Other composers represented were Martini, Fischer, Ricci, Hasse, Jomelli, Dr. Green, Worgan, Wilton, and Gossec.

The program announced June 24, 1786, was typical:

Act I.

Full Symphony, Pasquali

Song, Mr. Incledon

Symphony, Abel

Song, Mr. Martyr

Overture, Atalanta, Handel

Song, Mrs. Wrighten

Full Symphony, Haydn

Song, Miss Leary

Organ Concerto, Mr. Hook

Song, Miss Barnet

Glee — "How Sweet How Fresh"

And a Catch, called "The Street"

Act II.

Song, Mrs. Martyr

Concerto Oboe, Mr. Parke

Song, Mrs. Wrighten

Finale — Triumph of Beauty — Hook

Doors to be opened at Half past Six O'clock The Concert to begin at Eight. Admittance ONE SHILLING as usual.

London music activities always accelerated after the turn of the year. Not only did the Italian Opera at the King's Theatre, the English operas at Drury Lane and Covent Garden, the oratorios ushering in the Lenten season, and the subscription and membership concerts at various Rooms and Halls quicken, but dozens of benefit concerts were spliced into this busy schedule; frequently, several benefits were scheduled for the same evening. Instrumentalists -- or singers, or actors, or managers --- hoped, by carefully planning music for their programs and by thoughtfully choosing from among friends those performers who would attract a large audience, that "their night" would be a success financially as well as artistically.

On the whole, benefits followed the usual structure of two acts, an instrumental piece to open and close the concert, with vocal and instrumental music alternating. Orchestral music abounded. It is no surprise to find Haydn's music the most frequently played — on thirty-five out of fifty programs examined. Pleyel's name appeared seventeen times; for sixteen benefits, music of J. C. Bach was played, including eight performances of a "Grand Overture, Double Orchestra, M.S." (or "Symphony, Double Orchestra"). Cramer's January 8, 1788 benefit and Salomon's

March 11, 1788 concert both opened with a Mozart "Overture." Other composers frequently heard included Handel, Geminiani, Gluck, Corelli, Tartini from the older school and Rosetti, Raimondi, Giardini, Abel, Barthelemon and Arne from the "contemporary" composers. Salomon's benefit program is typical of these concerts:

Act I

    Overture, Mozart Quartetto, Pleyel
    Song, Mr. Harrison
    Concerto Flute, Mr. Graeff
    Duetto, Miss Abrams
    Concerto Violin, Mr. Salomon

Act II

    Overture, Clementi
    Concerto Piano Forte, Guedon
    Song, Mr. Harrison
    Concerto Oboe, Signor Caffaro (from Napolis)
    Song, Mrs. Billington
    Symphony, Haydn

Plainly the concerto, popular on most types of programs in this period, was a major item for the benefits. On the fifty programs examined, there were one hundred twelve concertos. The musician whose benefit it was always played at least one concerto.[29]

The violin and the oboe were the most popular solo instruments, but the French horn, the harp, and the flute were frequently heard. Fifteen piano forte concertos were played.[30] Such reputable soloists as Cramer, Parke, Huttley, Fischer, Ponto, the Leanders, Serjeant, and Cervetto appeared often on these concerts. Popular harpists, almost all of whom were women, included Mesdames Krumpholtz and La Roche, and Miss Denis. Abel, playing the viola da gamba, made his last public appearance at Mrs. Billington's concert, May 21, 1787.

Music performances for the benefit of the needy were a long tradition in England, and benefits for "causes" were plentiful in the period, 1785-1789. Many of these, such as the benefit for the "Royal Cumberland Freemasons School Instituted for the clothing, maintaining and education of Female Orphans, and Children of Free Masons,"[34] were under royal patronage. Directed by such figures as Cramer, Barthelemon, Dr. Arnold, and Dr. Cooke, these concerts attracted large audiences. Again, programs published by *The Times* showed Haydn to be a great favorite. On the May 25, 1789 concert, both his "New Overture, M.S. (in G)" and a "New Overture, M.S. (in F)." were played. In the preceding week for one of the Friday morning concerts "Under the patronage of Her Majesty for the Benefit of the General Lying-In Hospital," Cramer was leader of the band; Dr. Cooke was at the organ, and a full chorus performed the <u>Messiah</u>. At the end of Act I, Mme. Gautherot played a violin concerto, and at the end of Act II, Mme. Krumpholtz played a harp solo.

Private concerts were still another major musical activity in London during the 1785-1789 period. That patronage by members of the royal family and the nobility was a significant asset to any series of programs has been pointed out above. Their attendance at various musical functions was hailed in *The Times* columns with accounts of their presence, names of their entourage, descriptions of their attire. Attention was frequently called to the pleasures which they seemed to find in the music. Many members of these families were themselves good instrumentalists --- good amateurs --- and often performed for friends, alone or with professionals. Upon his first visit to London, Haydn, in several letters, refers to this interest in performance which he had observed. In a letter to Maria Anna Von Genziger, he wrote of a visit to "Oatlands," the country seat of the Duke of York; the Duchess, whom he found "delightful" and "very intelligent," played the pianoforte and sang "very nicely."[31] And, on another occasion, Haydn wrote of a two-day visit to the same villa where he and the Prince of Wales played music "for four hours in the evening ..."[32] W.T. Parke's memoirs record the Prince's interest in music and recall the rapidity of his progress with the violoncello under the tutelage of John Crosdill.[33]

Frequently the great houses were the scenes of more

formal concerts --- mornings and evenings --- with professional groups performing. Among the most notable of these were the Prince's parties at the Carlton House. *The Times* reporter observed on May 5, 1786: "The Prince's musical parties are now generally in the morning, but without company. He is too great an amateur to suffer the buz of conversation to interrupt the harmony of his concerts, which are, without exception, the best on a small scale perhaps in Europe; and when we mention the names Cramer, Crosdill and Schroeter where can such a trio be heard?" As reported by *The Times,* January 12, 1787, these occasions were "chiefly devoted to the quartettos of Haydn, Pleyel, Stamitz and the charming trios of Schroeter." On a more extended scale, other concerts were held at the Carlton House in the evenings. These, Parke wrote, "were entirely instrumental and might without impropriety be termed chamber-music." *The Times* noticed these concerts, too. But the Prince of Wales' concerts were only one such series. In the first month of *The Times'* publication, a column labeled "Musical Intelligence" twice carried a long account of a private "grand concert" in other noble households. The first of these was presented at the Duke of Queensborough's residence and was reported on January 11, 1785.

Concerto, violin, Mr. Lolli
Concerto, viol da gambo, Mr. Abel
Concerto, harpsichord, Mr. Schroeder

Concerto, violin, Mr. Cramer

Concerto, violin, Mr. Salomon

Concerto, oboe, Mr. Parke

Quartetto, in which Mr. Salomon led

Solo, on the violin, Mr. Lolli, Overture

On the 17th of January at Lord Brudenell's concert,

The performers were Messrs. Abel, Cramer, Crosdill, Zuck, Borgi, Parke, &. Lolli played a concerto and solo; the latter he performed in a stile more pleasing than usual. Abel was perfection. The duetto by Cramer and Crosdill was performed inimitably well; and amongst a number of well-chosen pieces, Mr. Zuck introduced, by desire of his Royal Highness, that charming Oboe Sestetto (a manuscript of the celebrated Bach) which he executed with the greatest delicacy and taste. The Adagio was performed in a stile of superior excellence, which shows Mr. Zuck a perfect master of the instrument, and a most valuable acquisition to the musical world.

Concerts at Buckingham, characterized by "excellent taste" or a "spirited plan," were frequently noted in *The Times*. Lord Chesterfield's Sunday Evening Concerts (Cramer led the band) were duly reported, as were those at Lord Hampden's and at Marlborough House. On April 1, 1788, Lord Uxbridge was said to be "fitting-up" his Music-Room for the opening of his grand concerts. Amateurs mingled with professionals for many of these musicales. When the Earl of Sandwich entertained his friends and neighbours at Hinchinbroke with music, "Miss Augusta Montagu's singing and brilliant and steady performance on the harpsichord, gave great delight to all who heard her. My Lord accompanied thorough bass on the harpsichord, in the full pieces, except such as had a part for the kettle-drums."[34]

One specific group of these private programs was called the "Ladies Concerts." In his Memoirs, Parke recalls playing for these, a gathering of men and women "of the highest class," and then he adds that the members were "superior Judges of music." These musical entertainments at the Duke of Queensberry's residence and at Lady Moore's were noted by *The Times*. At the last concert of the 1787 season, held at the Duchess of Marlborough's residence, Cramer, again, was leader of the band, Crosdill, "a principal performer;" Madame Mara sang, and Miss Denis played the harp.

Interest in private concerts was not limited to the nobility. On March 24, 1788, *The Times* reported that "the concert at Mr. Hammersly, the banker's on Thursday evening" was "one of the best appointed of any private entertainment this season." Cramer led the band, and among the performers was Miss Hammersly who played the harpsichord. For the Honorable Mrs. North's concert at Winchester House, noted June 12, 1788, "The first performers, vocal and instrumental, were engaged. Miss North performed a Sonata of Haydn on the Piano Forte. The whole was under the direction of Dr. Burney."

As has been shown, the reporters for *The London Times* followed with avid interest and enthusiasm the numerous,subscription, membership, and private concerts which were being performed in the various Rooms, Halls, Gardens, and great houses. Most of these programs were supplied with ample first-page advertisement preceding the scheduled performances. Notes, reviews, or critiques followed many of these concerts --- private and public. Of all forms of musical entertainment during this period, the instrumental concerts prompted the most consistently favorable response. The efforts of a band were usually rewarded with such terms of praise as "remarkably fine" or "truly superlative" or "beautifully sublime." Selection of the pieces was judged most often to deserve "the highest credit," the choices demonstrating the "good taste and judgment" of the directors or managers.

In almost all of these reviews, performances by outstanding individuals were singled out for praise. Cramer, Clementi, Parke,

Cervetto seemed invariably to distinguish themselves in a "brilliant manner." The "elegant stile" of Parke was frequently pointed out, and Cervetto's "admirable manner of accompanying recitatives" on the violoncello was greatly esteemed. Fischer, an eminent oboist, was distinguished for his "ravishing dexterity," his "delicacy and pathos," and his "correct counterpoint." "Fine tones" and a "brilliant shake" were observed in Ponto's French horn solos. One critic admired his method of "varying his notes in a peculiar manner by keeping one of his hands in the mouth of the horn while he is playing." The Leander brothers, also French horn players, were "unrivalled" in playing duettos, but lacked "the judgment and execution" of Pieltain, a member of the Prince's band. Mahon, a highly regarded clarinetist, played cadences which were "both learned and affecting in a high degree." Mahon, Huttley (oboe), and Potter (flute) were frequently mentioned for their fine accompaniments. Serjeant, who played the trumpet, was often commended, and Decamp was thought to be "superior to any of his contemporaries" on the German flute. The "Herculean" Gariboldi astonished his hearers with the "thunder" of his double bass.

There were excellent instrumentalists among the ladies, too, especially on the harp, an instrument much admired by *The Times* gamba critics. Mme. Krumpholtz was acclaimed by *The Times*, for "her style, taste, and execution," and Miss Dents was complimented for her "dexterity and sweetness" giving "great satisfaction to the lovers of that instrument." Among the amateurs performing in private concerts, the Duchess of Devonshire was "excellent" on the harp; Mrs. Thickness was said to be "second only to Abel" on the viola da gamba, and Mrs. Bradyll was praised for "a very brilliant merit" on the "Grand Piano Forte."

Muzio Clementi was recognized as the preeminent harpsichordist, pianofortist, and teacher of the day.[35] A *Times* critic, calling particular attention to a performance of one of his sonatas for an Anacreontic meeting, noted that Clementi "introduced an extempore Capriccio, which for taste, and execution exceeded anything we ever heard from him before." Among the gifted pupils of Clementi was Johann Baptist Cramer (called "Cramer, jun." by *The Times*), who appeared at various times on many of the programs covered in this study. One reporter declared that this young pianofortist promised "to rival the eminent masters of the present age. His taste is already no less chaste than his execution is brilliant and correct." Upon another occasion, however, a reviewer chided him for "the frequent introductions of rapid passages, which are extraneous to the subject, and often times intrude upon it. Mr. Cramer needs not this assistance, brilliant as it is, to establish his character as a masterly performer of the first rank."[36]

One of the most accomplished violinists of the day, Johann Peter Salomon, highly regarded for his "perfect possession of the finger board," was consistently praised for the mastery exhibited in his performances. A *Times* reviewer epitomized Salomon's reputation when he wrote that Salomon's name was "well established for his professional talents as well as his private good character ... (He) has been long at the top of his profession and is perhaps exceeded by no one in the kingdom for execution on the violin."[37]

Wilhelm Cramer, father of the young pianofortist, was one of the most renowned musicians of the day, greatly admired both as a violinist and as a leader of the major bands, including the Prince's. Elements in his playing chosen for special commendation were his "neatness and taste" and his "tone production." One perceptive listener noted that "he plays the passages . . . exactly as they are written." Another reviewer made this observation after he had heard one of Cramer's performances of a concerto: "whatever the critic could conceive of fire, gracefulness, or articulation, was outdone by this consummate master of his art."[38]

A close reading of *The London Times*, 1785-1789, reveals audiences, large, informed, lively, and actively interested in instrumental music; performers, gifted, accomplished, and busy in their professional engagements; and abundant music, old and new, readily accessible. Much of the music and many of the performers continue to occupy significant places in music history.

Instrumental performances during these years were successfully competing for audiences in a world crowded with vocal and choral productions. Numerous subscription series, membership-society programs, summer park concerts, benefits, and the innumerable private musicales --- all attracted an appreciable share of the London musical audience. This study of instrumental programs has shown that symphonies, "overtures," and concertos were the most popular forms of instrumental music, and further, has indicated that there was a considerable interest in ensemble and chamber music: duettos, trios, quartettos, and quintets for various combinations of instruments. With excellent music composed for it and played by able musicians, the pianoforte was rapidly growing in popularity, being often heard in concertos, as an accompanying instrument, and in solo performances.

The Times' accounts demonstrate that contemporary instrumental music was even more popular than the works of the older composers. When they did choose "old music" for their programs, the concert directors showed a preference for such enduring composers as Pergolesi, Geminiani, Corelli, Boyce, Byrd, and Handel. The strong interest in contemporary music was manifested in the repeated performances of the music of Haydn, Mozart, J. C. Bach, Stamitz, and other highly regarded composers of the day. Recurrent appearances of these old and new works in so many highly varied concert settings suggest that the public largely shared the musical taste of managers and performers.

Critics, for their part, paid a great deal of attention to the performers, and their reactions indicated a sensitivity to technique, style, and professional achievement. Band leaders and directors were recognized for their various contributions, and eminent instrumentalists, as well as many of lesser fame, found their professional renown reinforced by the consistent attention given them in the reporters' columns.

In his <u>Musical Memoirs</u>, W. T. Parke noted that by 1784 instrumental music in London had "arrived at a high degree of perfection." The activities of the subsequent five years (1785-1789), as revealed in the illuminating columns of *The London Times*, fully justify the accolade which Parke paid his fellow musicians.

FOOTNOTES

[1]Marion M. Scott, "Haydn in England," Musical Quarterly, 18 (April 1932), 262.

[2]Karl Geiringer, Haydn (Berkeley and Los Angeles: University of California Press, 1968), p. 101.

[3]This chapter in London's music history is treated in detail in Charles Sanford Terry's John Christian Bach (2nd edition: London, New York, Toronto: Oxford University Press, 1967), pp. 90-96.

[4]Gallini later bought out Bach and Abel. Further details may be found in Terry, pp. 140-143.

[5]W. T. Parke, Musical Memoirs (London: Henry Colburn and Richard Bentley, 1830), I, 53.

[6]February 23, 1785; 1-1. An error in reporting or in printing this program seems likely. The concerto and duetto were probably played by Messrs. Leander, popular French horn players, and may have been composed by Bach.

[7]Landon points out that in 1774 a London performance of a symphony, probably No. 53, was "supposed to have taken place." H. C. Robbins Landon, The Symphonies of Joseph Haydn (London: Universal Edition and Rockliff, 1955), p. 366. Nettel, less specific, suggests the first appearance of Haydn's name in England as being "on Bach and Abel's programmer." Reginald Nettel, The Orchestra in England (London: Jonathon Cape, 1946), p. 80. Young also mentions the inclusion of Haydn's music "on the Bach-Abel programmes." Percy M. Young, A History of British Music (New York: W. W. Norton and Company, 1967), p. 389.

[8]Distinctions between the terms "overture," "symphony," "full piece," "grand overture," "divertemente," and the like, as they appeared on the programs in the newspapers are not always clear. The question of terminology for types of music as used in the late eighteenth century is an involved one.

[9]Since compositions are seldom identified precisely, one cannot know how frequently these numbers are repeated from program to program.

[10]January 24, 1787; 1-2. An almost identical list of the perform-

ers, without instrumental assignments, had appeared on December 10, 1785. Variant spellings of musicians' names frequently appear in *The Times*.

[11]An excellent history and description of this hall is to be found in Robert Elkin's The Old Concert Rooms of London (London: Edward Arnold, 1955), pp: 65-71.

[12]November 28, 1786; 1-2.

[13]Elkin, p. 106.

[14]Announcements for membership Society concerts were never published on the first page of *The Times* where advance notices of public entertainment were always to be found.

[15]Elkins, p. 105.

[16]This is the only instance in which Salomon was mentioned as the "leader" of the Academy of Antient Music band; on all other occasions Barthelemon was named as leader.

[17]William Sandys and Simon Andrew Forster, The History of the Violin (London: William Reeves, 1864), p. 177.

[18]For an account of these rooms, see Elkins, pp. 82-91.

[19]Charles Burney, A General History of Music from the Earliest Ages to the Present Period (1789), a new edition with Critical and Historical Notes by Frank Mercer (2 vols.; London: Foulis; New York: Harcourt, 1935; New York: Dover Publications, 1957), II, 1022.

[20]Parke, I, 55. According to Elkins, this band consisted of "sixteen violins, five violas, four violoncellos, two double basses, four oboes, four horns, two trumpets, three trombones and timpani." Elkins, p. 84.

[21]An exception is to be found in the announcements of the six Fridays during Lent when oratorios were performed under the direction of the Ancient Concerts. Ample space was devoted to these performances, and reviews and notices were enthusiastic.

[22]November 17, 1787; 3-1.

[23]Parke, I, 81.

[24]February 1, 1788; 3-2.

[25]November 9, 1787; 3-1.

[26]This work is probably K498, Trio for Piano, Clarinet, and Viola in E flat.

[27]Illustrious guests at Ranelagh included Wolfgang Amadeus Mozart, who at the age of ten performed there on the harpsichord and organ, and twenty-eight years later his friend, Franz Joseph Haydn, who attended Giardini's benefit on May 21, 1792. H. C. Robbins Landon, The Collected Correspondence and London Notebooks of Joseph Haydn (London: Barrie and Rockliff, 1959), p. 257.

[28]Mollie Sands, Invitation to Ranelagh, 1742-1803 (London: John Westhouse, 1946).

[29]The violinist and composer, Raimondi, planned his May 19, 1788 benefit to include, out of six instrumental pieces, an overture and a grand symphony of his own composition, a concerto played by himself, and a duet composed for violin and tenor, which he performed with Cramer.

[30]On seven programs, pianoforte sonatas were played by such performers as Clementi; Cramer, Junior; Dusseck, Miss Abrams, Miss Parke, and Miss Barthelemon.

[31]Landon, Correspondence, p. 123.

[32]Ibid., p. 272.

[33]Parke, II, 319.

[34]January 6, 1786; 2-4.

[35]An exception to those critics and musicians who were impressed by Clementi's virtuosity was Mozart who thought him to be "a mere mechanicus" with "...not a farthing's worth of taste or feeling." From a letter partially quoted by Alfred Einstein, Mozart (New York: Oxford University Press, 1965), p. 237.

[36]December 21, 1787; 2-3.

[37]March 13, 1788; 3-4.

[38]September 30, 1788; 3-4.

About the Author

Sarah Joiner Wynn was born in Helena - McRae, Georgia, but some ten years later, her family moved to Savannah, then and still --- an enchanting city to live in. After high school, she entered the University of Georgia, graduating with her B.A. degree in English; but throughout all of the preceding years, with fine teachers and encouraging parents, she very seriously studied and "practiced" piano! Upon graduation, she taught public school music in Savannah.

Not long after this new venture, friends suggested an interesting summer venture. "Let's go to Duke!" So away they went and along with hard, hard work toward an M.A. degree in English, a wonderful summer (with several more summers following!)

Part of the "wonderfulness" was the coincidence of another person there from Georgia "for the summer" --- an English teacher, Lawrence Wynn: "Yes" and several summers passed and degrees were earned.

For his part - he was continuing his B.A. from Emory to his M.A. from Duke to plan for entrance to Princeton for his doctorate.

War years intervened, and plans for all Americans changed. But for them their plans were finalized, and they were married while he was serving in the U.S. Navy as an ensign. After the war, Princeton again, and after his Ph.D. degree from there, to Memphis State. (Now, the University of Memphis)

And Sarah? Upon settling down in Memphis, private piano teaching and further interests in scholastic expansion in music: a B.M. degree, and then the M.M. degree at the University. She is an active member of the Beethoven Club in Memphis and serves on the Board of Directors. Also a member of the Tennessee Music Teachers Association, she was recently awarded the "Teacher of the Year" distinction by the Memphis Association.

111

Design, Typography and Production by
Langford & Associates
3307 Park Avenue
Memphis, Tennessee 38111
901.324.8769   Fax 901.458.4151